D1684922

Touring Guide

COPENHAGEN

Get to know it — get to like it

by
Horst Fuchs

English translation and adaptation by Karl Westenberger

Published by
Drake Publishers Inc.   New York
and
Interauto Book Co., Ltd.   London

1

Drake Publishers Inc.
381 Park Avenue South,
New York, N.Y., U.S.A.

Library of Congress Cataloging in Publication
Data.
Drake Publishers. Drake touring guide,
Copenhagen. 1. Copenhagen--Description--
Guide-books. I. Title. DL276.A4D7 1973
914.89'1 73-5827.
ISBN 0-87749-534-3

U.K. and Commonwealth Edition
Interauto Book Company Limited
Bercourt House
51 York Road
Brentford, Middlesex, England.
ISBN 0-903192-49-7

© Interauto Book Co. Ltd. 1973

Original German edition
"KOPENHAGEN KENNEN UND LIEBEN"
Published by LN-Verlag, Luebeck, Germany

© LN-Verlag 1972

Drawings by Howard Williams

Printed in England by
HGA Printing Company Ltd.
Brentford, Middlesex.

CONTENTS

The changing of the guard at the Amalienborg Palace.

CHAPTER 1

WHAT IS COPENHAGEN?

This city has many features, and that also applies to its' women. What does this mean? A city is something alive which opens itself at once to some, to others only after some hesitation or to a few never at all. Is it an institution of dwelling, working, living, loving; or is it a partnership of joint interests, a getto, or even a monster?

It is certainly a little of everything. Everyone has to find his own interpretation. One should in any case attempt to come to close terms with a particular city. After all, eighty per cent of the people will be living in cities on the European continent by the year 2000. No harm therefore to adapt oneself to this situation in time. In the case of Copenhagen many people have come to close terms, this is a cosmopolitan city which in this respect does not know any national boundaries. Everybody is welcome although it may have more to offer to some than to others.

There is of course in a true city such a wide range of contrasting things from tarmac boilers to toffee boilers, dustbins to greenhouses, castles and public conveniences, windy corners and long-stretching promenades. Anyhow all this does exist in Copenhagen.

Copenhagen is a city of superlatives: It has the most famous "Langelinie" (promenade) in the world, the biggest Danish newspaper of the world is published in Copenhagen, and there is a butcher in the city who has a sign above his shop: "You get the world's best bacon here". This is another feature of this city, the ability to smile sarcastically at itself, but nonetheless to regard itself as something extraordinary and great. In the case of the butcher this means that nobody can disprove his claim to have the world's best bacon, nobody has any reason to do so either, for Danish bacon is the world's best, or is it? Besides, is this Copenhagen rule: Anything that gives fun and enjoyment is permitted.

Getting to like Copenhagen is easy indeed, all that is required on your part is to be ready for it. Getting to know Copenhagen is somewhat more difficult. And to write about it is even more of a problem. There is another feature, or rather features, of this city, namely those of its women. They, too, are difficult to encompass under a common denominator so surprisingly varied is their appearance. These features range from improvised elegance, instead of a button on a blouse, a flower, paper clip or nothing, to the cheroot-puffing matron displaying a mixture of arrogance and emancipation.

And women are but a small part of this big city, though not the minor one, just small.

CHAPTER 2

AT FIRST GLANCE

You can get to like Copenhagen also without women. First you will have to ask yourself where Copenhagen is and how to get there. After all there are still some people in the world who associate the word Copenhagen primarily with Danny Kaye who was the first to sing the song about wonderful Copenhagen. This was when he took the part of Hans Christian Andersen who once upon a time lived in Copenhagen, wrote fairy tales, narrated them himself and who today is sitting on a pedestal beside the town hall. Others again may think, Copenhagen and the famous international treaty, which sets out and specifies the various wave lengths allocated to radio stations all over the world. And there are those who may be tempted to a glass of Danish lager which has become very popular over here and in other countries. You can of course fly to Copenhagen from Britain and many other major cities on the European continent.

Alternatively you can travel by rail and cross by ferry, for instance, coming from England via the port of

Esbjerg on the west coast of Jutland. From elsewhere in Scandinavia you make your approach via Øresund on the doorsteps of Copenhagen. And there is another train route to Copenhagen which once was the most essential link with the European continent, namely Berlin — Warnemünde — Gedser — Copenhagen. There is now only one express train a day from the East German railway system which in most cases is empty and is taken across from Warnemünde to Gedser by a Danish ferry or one of the "Deutsche Reichsbahn" ferries. The ferry boats operate several times a day.

On the Hamburg — Lübeck — Puttgarden — Rødby — Copenhagen route there are 30 express trains a day during the main season, outside the season there are a "mere" 20. These trains come from, and go to, almost every major city in Western Europe.

Since Copenhagen is situated on the island of Zealand, you can virtually arrive in front of your hotel by boat. Direct connections exist with Great Britain, the USA, Canada, Sweden, Norway, Finland, Iceland.

From Malmö in Sweden the ferry takes 100 minutes, hydrofoils cross the "Sound" within 35 minutes. If you come from Germany, there is a boat service from Lübeck-Travermünde which takes a night, or eight hours during day time, and from Travermünde to Gedser takes three hours. The remaining 90 miles to Copenhagen are easy to cover either by rail or by road, or even on a bicycle. In the latter case there are a few climbs in the rolling south of Zealand, apart from this it is a smooth and clear "ride".

Last but not least there are internal Danish boat services between Copenhagen and the Färo Isles, Greenland, Jutland and Bornholm. Whether you make your approach by air, sea or road, our City soon becomes perceptible as something extraordinary.

The big jet airliners start their descent before Denmark has even come into sight. If you are lucky, and the sky is clear, you will soon see the built up areas becoming more dense, the towns and suburbs growing, the lines hardening into roads and streets and the ant-like specks turning into cars. And there she is, the big City, only to disappear again and you stare down onto water, the

aeroplane goes into it's final bend and you land on the island of Amager, at Kastrup airport.

A particularly impressive view opens up in front of you if you approach Copenhagen on a night flight. First the horizon brightens up, then many lights appear on both sides of the Sound because Malmö "on the other side" is also a major town. But Copenhagen is unmistakenly identifiable by a huge index finger, floodlit in red colour, at the city centre: the obelisk of the Carlsberg brewery.

The approach by boat is less abrupt, more leisurely. You pass by the white cliffs of Møn, then you enter the wide bay of Køge to find a rather amazing outpost of the big city, namely the fishermen's village of Dragør at the tip of Amagar island; immediately after this you pass the airport where touch-down and take-off goes on throughout the day. Be patient we are still not there. The oil harbour and military installations which have yet to be negotiated. And then there it is, a skyline of sights from the distant and more recent past. The new overshadows the old, the highest construction is Copenhagen's Gladsaxe Television tower (267 metres above sea level) looks down on all. Other predominant landmarks of the silhouette are also of a more technological character: Svanemøllen power station with its three chimneys and the H.C. Ørsted plant with seven, the Gladsaxe gasometer and the Maersk refineries, also the telephone exchange tower, Copenhagen's "Post Office tower". But the latter, only just overshadows the 105 metre town hall and also the Frederiksberg town hall which is of a later date, but unfortunately is also less attractive. It surmounts the "skyscrapers" among which four big hotels are at the top in various respects: SAS-Hotel Royal, Tre Falke, Europa and Copenhagen.

Nonetheless the most enchanting landmarks continue to be the old towers and spires: the green spire of the church of Our Saviour with a curious spiral staircase winding around it, sparkling in a golden colour, 86,60 metres high, built 1747-1752. The Christiansborg with the three crowns one upon another, are not far from the Baroque tower of Copenhagen's oldest church, St. Peter. Beside it you discover the square tower of the Classicist cathedral, officially referred to as "Our Dear Lady". Then there is St. Nikolaj church whose spire, or at least its tip, was a donation by the brewery owner Carl Jacobsen. Very impressive to many foreign visitors is the dome of Frederik's church in the Roman Baroque style, completed in 1894, which looks as if it had been modelled on Rome's St. Peter. Grundtvig's church with its lofty brick façade is something special, it is very similar to the typical Danish village churches. The church is in the north of the city, at Copenhagen's highest point, namely Bispebjerg (Bishop's hill), 34 metres above sea level. We must also mention at this stage the Round Tower in the city centre which, though only 34 metres high, is 300 years old. It contains a viewing platform and an observatory open to the public. A totally different silhouette of Copenhagen appears when you look from the Sound, a view which is very much tuned to the farewell mood which overcomes you as you leave the city by night, which then eventually vanishes into the Sound. At this time, strings of lights, small ones and big ones, reflected by the water light-up along the coast in many colours. If you leave in a northerly direction, the whole vast projection of the city becomes evident once again, the almost continuous chain of lights stretches as far as Helsingør, at the same time you can see the Swedish coast lit-up some 30 miles away. This view gives us some idea of what the economists mean when they talk of areas of congestion, in this case the Øre-Sound region.

The least disturbing way to approach Copenhagen is by rail. Soon after having boarded the train, whether from Helsingør, Korsøor or Rødby, the traveller can prepare himself at leisure without having to watch traffic, traffic lights, speed limits, roaming cows or wild moped riders.

At first, as you look out of your train window, you are confronted with the entire spectrum of Danish scenery: brown-red cows on green pastures, straight and smooth tarmac roads cut through meadows and fields, lined with farmhouses glaring in spotless cleanliness with long-stretching roofs and lots of flowers in front of them. There are also some towns along the route where idyllic features alternate with modern ones, cottages on the one hand and present-day apartment blocks on the other hand.

Gradually blocks of flats grow wider, and houses higher, factory buildings and warehouses with gigantic advertisement posters emerge, brown metropolitan trains run in a shuttle service, signs with the names of suburban railway stations fly past, suddenly your train is right in the middle of a jungle of houses and buildings, and eventually rolls into the main station, called by the locals, 'Hovedbanegaarden', which is an ideal opportunity to the foreigner to practise Danish pronounciation; it is much easier to say Central Station.

CHAPTER 3

THE CAPITAL

What are the criteria by which to define a capital? In a capital, there is Parliament, Government, Supreme Court of Justice, big organisations have their head office here, there are major cultural institutions, there is a city press, broadcasting and television stations and studios. A true capital is a big city, in many cases the biggest city of the respective country. All of this applies to Copenhagen.

Copenhagen is Denmark's biggest city; yet it is not all that simple to establish how big it is. You are quoted from one source a population of 1.5 million, others will say 700,000. To sort out this discrepancy we first must clarify the concept of Copenhagen. The 1.5 million Copenhageners — which would amount to a third of the population, live in Copenhagen and the twenty surrounding boroughs. The outskirts and neighbouring towns are fully independent and would not dream of becoming integrated with the borough of Copenhagen. Even right in the middle of the city of Copenhagen there is such an independent body: Frederiksberg. As you walk a few hundred yards to the west from Copenhagen's main railway station you have already left the city, and are in Frederiksberg. To the visitor that may not matter at all, but to the inhabitants of Frederiksberg it means a lot, for they pay less tax in wealthy Frederiksberg than others do in "poorer" Copenhagen. Frederiksberg council rates are lower because the area comprises mainly residential districts which in former times were classed as "posh". And since overall inland revenue takings are higher here, one can afford lower rates than are imposed upon less affluent citizens. Also the visitor becomes aware that he is in Frederiksberg because here the kerb-stones at the street corners are sloping and flattened so as to make it easier for prams to be wheeled-on and off. This is not so in Copenhagen.

Telephone kiosks in Frederiksberg are red, in Copenhagen they are green. They even have a fire brigade and town hall of their own in Frederiksberg. The remaining neigh-bouring boroughs of Copenhagen are outskirts in the proper sense of the word, in the north is Gentofte, another big and "posh" borough with a population of 100,000. Gentofte operates a special co-operative scheme with the Copenhagen bus and streetcar transport system; one uses the same coaches but at the borough border you pay once more, this time to the other corporation, don't worry you don't have to get out of your seat. The same applies when you go to the city from the isle of Amagar, say from Kastrup airport. Other outskirts have a bus service of their own, in most cases called Rutebiler, which take you as far as the borough border where you change to the Copenhagen metropolitan lines.

The quickest way to cross the city and get far out into the surrounding countryside as far as Klampenborg and Holte in the north or Ballerup and Tastrup in the west is by Bybane, the S-trains. The longest line of this network operated by Danish railways extends 10 miles beyond the city limits; the electrified S-train system was built in 1934, the respective stations are marked by a capital S in red.

A capital is identifiable by its Government District rather than its bus and tram system. In Copenhagen this district is on an island, namely Slotsholmen. The most important and highest building is the Christiansborg Palace, seat of the Folketing, the parliament, the Foreign Office and the Supreme Court, also housing reception

The Town Hall

chambers of the royal family. Here the King, or as it is now, the Queen, sits in council with the government once a week. The present-day Christiansborg Palace did not come about until 1907 to 1928. It is the sixth Christiansborg to have been erected on this site.

First a fortress was built in the 12th century which was destroyed by foreign invaders, and then reconstructed by the people of Copenhagen. Its ruins can be seen under the present building. In the early 15th century a new palace became the first royal residence. Later on this was pulled-down by order of Christian VI. During 1733 to 1745 the first really stately palace was erected, this went up in flames in 1794, when the royal family moved to Amalienborg where they or rather their successors continue to live nowadays.

The funds for the next Christiansborg were raised by the Danes in a nationwide collection. The new palace was completed in 1828 only to burn down in 1884.

Building material from all over Denmark was used for the present-day Christiansborg. The facade is made of Bornholm granite, for the ground floor around the parliament square and the foundations of the Riding School in the north wing, 600 free-stones were used from the 600 boroughs of Denmark. Sculpture faces look down from the windows, they are faces of Danish politicians of those times.

Christiansborg belongs to the people, it has been the seat of the parliament since 1918, and the constitution is kept in a silver shrine in the lobby of the Folketing.

Apart from the main hall for the 179 members of parliament there is also a canteen for hard-working politicians, which is referred to colloquially as "Snapsting" although there is hardly any snaps drunk here. The word snapsting has become part of the official Danish dictionary, even the prime minister uses it.

The palace church on the north side of the main building is also part of Christiansborg, this is a classical piece of architecture by C.F. Hansen. The angels in the cupola of the chapel are a work by Thorvaldsen. The church was consecrated in 1826.

Behind the Christiansborg chapel, between the palace and the canal, rises a monumental building, namely Thorvaldsen's Museum. The rectangular building in its' bright yellow is by colour and shape a distinctive contrast to the grey palace. It also has a history of its own.

Bertel Albert Thorvaldsen, born in 1770, had spent forty years of his life in Rome before he returned to his home town Copenhagen in 1838. He was rated as the most eminent sculptor of his time and he was received like a prince when he came back.

On the 5th December 1838, Thorvaldsen signed a document in which he donated to his native city all his life work, no matter whether they were originals or copies, even some marble statues, also his enormous collections of contemporary paintings, Egyptian, Greek and Roman antiques as well as his entire remaining estate. The only condition he made, was that a museum was to be built to accommodate these works. The building was completed in 1848, four years after Thorvaldsen's death. The sculptor was buried here, surrounded by all his works; but had at least lived to see and approve the design of the building which had been by the architect Gottlieb Bindesbøll.

In those days the museum amounted to a sensation. Thorvaldsen's statues were placed against the background of coloured walls, the decor of the ceilings was modelled on Pompeiian styles, and the outer facade was given a gigantic pictorial mural by the painter Jørgen Sonne who, using colour-soaked mortar 1/8 inch thick, depicted the return of the artist from Rome in 1838 and the transporting of his works from the steamer to the museum. The faces on the frieze are portraits of prominent Danes of that period.

An inscription on the façade reads: "This work was completed in 1848, thanks to the joint efforts of King Frederik VI and King Christian VIII, the borough of Copenhagen and citizens from all walks of life".

The outer frieze was given a total face lift during 1949 to 1958 and the museum now radiates the bright colours as in the days when it was first built.

In front of the main gate to the Christiansborg palace,

which is hardly ever opened because visitors use a smaller side entrance, an equestrian statue of King Frederik VII was erected in 1873. As you can read in Danish history books he relinquished in March 1848 "under moderate pressure of public opinion" his right of absolute rule which had existed in the country since 1660. It was a typically Danish revolution. Whilst in Paris and Berlin bullets were fired and blood flowed freely on the continent, in Copenhagen, some citizens exercised "moderate pressure of public opinion" in that they went to see their king suggesting that he should give them a liberal constitution, to which he agreed. A national assembly drew-up a constitution which was signed by Frederik on the 5th June, 1849 and thus became the initiator of the Danish Bill of Rights, which made Denmark a constitutional monarchy. The king had chosen the 5th of June for his signature because his mistress's son was eight years old on that day. This mistress was the ballet dancer and "boutique" owner Louise Rasmussen. The king made her Countess Danner and she made herself the country's First Lady. The relationship between the king and this "commoner" added considerably to his popularity with the people of Copenhagen.

The new constitution was labelled "June Constitution" and it was at the time one of the most liberal constitutions in Europe. There were to be two "houses", the Folketing and the Landsting. All Danish men above the age of thirty were given electoral right, the king could no longer govern without his ministers, and judiciary power was placed into the hands of independent courts of justice.

On the other side of Christiansborg, within the vast inner courtyard which opens to the south-west, we find another monument of a king. This time Christian IX who was considered very important. He was often referred to as Europe's father-in-law because four of his children had ascended to European thrones. His successor was his son Frederik who took the title of Frederik VIII, Alexandra was married to King Edward VII of England, Vilhelm became King George I of Greece and Dagmar married Czar Alexander III. His grandson Carl, Frederik VIII's second-eldest son, was elected King of Norway in 1905 and took the title of Haakon VII. Christian who reigned from 1863 to 1906, had a lot of trouble with the parliament or rather a quarrel with the two parliamentary houses "Folketing" and "Landsting". Basically it was about the introduction of parliamentary democracy in Denmark. The assembly hall of the Landsting in the old parliament building was considered above that of the Folketing; but this was not sheer coincidence because the Landsting was the "upper house". But in 1918 the new present-day parliament building of Christiansborg was erected and the "Landsting" was placed on the same level as the "Folketing".

Already under Christian IX the argument had been decided in favour of the Folketing which was elected by the people in direct and secret ballot. Christian's monument was not erected until 21 years after his death, in 1927.

The equestrian statue is the work by a lady artist, Anne Marie Carl-Nielsen. It is by the Riding School which is still used as such today. The royal horses are in the north wing of the palace. Whenever big events are imminent, state visits for instance, one can watch here the departure of the royal coach as it leaves for the Queen's residence.

The present Queen and her two sisters, Princess Benedikte and Princess Anne-Marie, used to have their riding lessons here, but their days of school have long come to an end and they have in the meantime had children of their own.

Opposite the north wing, that is in the south wing, we see the old Court Theatre dating back to 1766. Since 1922 it has been a Theatrical Museum. The site bears a certain significance with the fate of the German physicist Johann Friedrich Struensee. He was doctor, consultant, cabinet secretary and secret minister of King Frederik IV, and lover of young Queen Caroline Mathilde. When a fancy-dress party was held in the Court Theatre a conspiracy against him was successful and the king approved of Struensee's arrest. The minister was taken to the citadel as a prisoner, charged, sentenced and publicly tortured and executed in front of the Østerport "without uttering a single word of lament".

Within sixteen months Struensee had managed to enact some six hundred laws and made redundant a large number of civil servants. Some say his actions had been quite modern, they were equally dangerous as we see.

Caroline Mathilde, sister of England's King George III, was sent into exile at Celle where she died in 1775, only 24 years old.

There is more to the Government District than Christiansborg on Slotsholmen (palace island). Most of the ministeries have their offices here. A visitor who has seen other ministerial buildings in Europe will be impressed by the modesty with which Danish ministers have accommodated themselves. Their offices are just a single complex of buildings, in a quiet street, a few hundred yards long, which leads from Christiansborg to the harbour. Because of the colour of its face it is simply referred to as the "Red Building". The Red Building dates back to the period 1715-1720 and is in Baroque style. For some years an annex has been attached to it, a modern steel and concrete structure with large glass surfaces, an indication also in Denmark that ministerial bureaucracy is increasing. No less than 11 state departments or ministeries have their plaques at the entrance door. Architecturally speaking the most remarkable building on Slotsholmen island is the Børse, the Stock Exchange, a splendid example of Renaissance architecture, erected under King Christian IV, who was obsessed with building and who has left his marks in this respect at many other points of the city. It is claimed to be the oldest stock exchange in the world still used for its original purpose. The twisted tails of four dragons form it's spire. The big ballroom, which is open to the public, dates back to 1856/7. The offices of the Copenhagen Chamber of Commerce are also accommodated in this building.

On the harbour side of Slotsholmen is Tøhuset with the Royal Danish Armoury and Museum, built under Christian IV from 1598 to 1604. One wing of the building is justifiably referred to as the "Long Arsenal" because it contains one of the longest halls in Europe, 500 ft. long. The museum was installed in 1928. It contains numerous flags, uniforms, swords, cannons and other objects usually to be found in an armoury. The courtyard is decorated with a colossal cast iron lion which has a history of its own. Originally the "Idsted" lion guarded at the Flensburg cemetery, the graves of Danish soldiers who lost their lives during the "1848-1850 uprising" against the Schleswig-Holsteins. The Danes refer to these events as "uprising" because the Schleswig-Holsteins fought against their then ruler, the King of Denmark. After 1864, when Schleswig-Holstein had become part of Prussia, the lion came to the Crown Prince in Berlin. It was here that the Americans took him over in 1945, and returned the monument to Denmark where it has now found its place in front of the arsenal on Slotsholem island at Copenhagen. Two buildings which must be included in the skyline of this government district are not on Slotsholmen island, but right next door; they are the Holmens Kirke opposite the Stock Exchange and the National Museum behind the palace. Holmens Kirke was originally an anchor foundry for the royal navy. It was erected in 1563 and is the oldest Renaissance building in Copenhagen. In 1619 the foundry became a church and from 1641 to 1643 it was reconstructed and modified. Needless to mention that the commissioner was Christian IV. Holmens Kirke has a "Royal Gate" which once was part of Roskilde cathedral, and it continues to be the church of the royal family and the navy. Two of Denmark's greatest naval heroes are buried here; Niels Juel, the man who shredded the Swedish fleet at Køge in 1677, and the almost legendary Norwegian Peter Wessel who defeated Charles XII of Sweden during the Great Northern War, and was knighted by King Frederik IV whereupon he was renamed Tordenskjold (Thunder Shield).

The earliest part of the National Museum, the prince's palace, was not built under Christian IV. It dates back to 1684 and was originally a nobleman's mansion. Later on it became the residence of the crown prince who ascended to the throne as Frederik V. The extension by the canal opposite the court yard of Christiansborg was added during the 18th century. The arcades on the north side are only some forty years old.

The best way to end a stroll across and around Slotsholmen is to visit the gardens of the Royal Library, Bibliotekshaven, which you can reach through the Imperial Archives from the court yard of the Folketing. It is hard to describe the idyllic gardens with a term other than the somewhat cliché-like attribute "Oasis of Peace". The library itself contains Denmark's largest collection of books, newspapers, and ancient manuscripts, including the earliest records of Viking expeditions to America and Greenland. The architecture of the building which was completed in 1906, would be described as "Byzantine-Romaneque" but not without a few trappings in art nouveau. The second important site where Copenhagen manifests its character as a capital, though in a totally different manner than on Slotsholmen, is Town Hall Square, in Danish the "Raadhuspladsen".

The Town Hall was built from 1893 to 1905 by the architect Martin Nyrop. The decision to erect a town hall (the fifth in the city's history) on this site came about when Copenhagen's fortifications were demolished. Originally the west gate was here and after the demolition a marvellous space was available where Nyrop had at first erected a number of wooden buildings and pavilions for a great northern exhibition.

Nyrop's most favourite building materials were granite, bricks, chalk, copper and timber all of which were used for his Town Hall project. Parts of the architecture of the building reflect Danish mediaeval elements, but also the Italian Renaissance. The subjects of interior decor, were purely nordic however, no lions but polar bears, seals, sea gulls and crabs. High above the main entrance is the gilded figure of the founder of the city, Bishop Absalon, flanked by a fireman and a policeman. The town hall tower is 350 ft. high and from here you have fine views of the city and the surrounding countryside. It's carillon with the tune of the "old watchman's signal" can be heard in the whole of Denmark at precisely noon every day, it is also used by the Danish broadcasting corporation as a time signal.

Inside you can see a World Clock invented by Jens Olsen; the clock is said to lose only four seconds in 3000 years. It shows both the Julian and the Gregorian calendars and the respective stellar constellations and all eclipses of the moon and the sun. Jens Olsen had been building the clock for 27 years and he died before it had been fully installed, which alone took 10 years.

The master of the house in Town Hall is the Lord Mayor, there are also five burgermasters and five councillors who together form the city council. The municipal parliament has 55 delegates. You could describe the political situation of Copenhagen as perfectly stable, since 1917 the social domocrats have been the biggest party.

"Town Hall square provides the livelihood for the population of a medium-size provincial town," thus once wrote a playwright. He was right. You can buy sandwiches, sausages, fruit, pigeon food, theatre tickets, films, newspapers, frivolous and serious books, pictures, tram tickets, cigarettes and souvenirs of all descriptions in the square. You can have a rest, drink coffee, whisky or beer and underneath the square you can leave your suitcase, or have a wash and use the other facilities.

The square is buzzling with life at all times, everywhere you run into tourists; and yet it has managed to remain a square whose features and character are those of the locals. Whilst the tourists feed the pigeons, the Copenhageners look after the sparrows; the sausage stands are surrounded by solicitors, messenger boys, workers, directors, ladies and girls, one beside the other. They all eat the same pink sausages, called 'Viennese', grilled Pølser or even hamburgers.

The Smørrebrød stalls offer "mystery" packs for 6 Kr. or for 3 Kr. What is inside you will not find out until you unpack it. When several members of a family have made such "blindfold" buys an entertaining game may then take place: Swap liver paté for egg, etc.

You can read a newspaper very cheaply indeed on town hall square. You simply have to study "Politikens Lysavis", the illuminated newspaper, high above at the facade of the "Politiken" newspaper building, which runs continually along the roof. News and commercials alternate in an undisrupted cycle. After you have read Politikens Lysavis three or even five times, you may further improve your Danish by studying the numerous colourful advertisements with which the town hall square is flooded from all directions by night.

Another, rather sober, piece of information is displayed on the "Zero Stone" in front of the town hall. On this 5 ft. high granite block which stands on the site of the former West Gate, you can read the distance in kilometres to various towns in Zealand and the southern islands.

Radhuspladsen is also a forum for the Copenhagen people, not so much to conduct heated discussions, but to enjoy themselves. A most enchanting town hall square festival takes place on midsummer night when the Copenhageners dance on their square, which is literally called "dance on the tarmac".

The town hall is flanked by two monuments, on the east side two silent "Lur"-playing musicians stand on a high column, which gave the Danish butter its brand name "lurmarket smor": a "lur" on the butter pack means quality. The "lur" is a Bronze-age musical instrument, an odd-shaped "trumpet" which was popular some 3000 years ago. The "lurists" have never blown their instruments yet, but people say they will do so when a virgin passes-by below! On the other side of the town hall sits Hans Christian Andersen; immortalised in bronze, the great spinner of fairy tales gazes across the boulevard named after him, to Tivoli Gardens, the entertainment centre for little and grown-up children. It is not certain from the expression on his face whether he looks with longing or in deep reflection. Another monument of the playwright is in Kongens Have. His grave is at "Assistenz" cemetery. The dragon fountain in front of the town hall was erected in 1904, the centre portion of the basin is of a later date, 1923.

Also the tired pedestrian was considered within the layout of Town Hall square. Adjoining the Town Hall, by H.C. Andersen boulevard, is the Town Hall Garden with bench seats set amidst a mass of flowers.

The underground station beneath the square is also a pedestrian subway.

The traffic jams in the square last until 12.30 at night. At this time "the last buses leave from all corners of the square on their final run" to the outskirts of the city.

A special scene and atmosphere exists in the square during the pre-Christmas period. A huge Christmas tree is erected in front of the Town Hall, in most cases a gift from another Scandinavian city; apart from hot sausages and other victuals, typical Christmas items are on sale, for instance small goats made of straw, these are a typical Swedish Christmas decoration. Collections are organised for the poor and in front of the towering Christmas tree is a large glass case into which coins of all kinds of currency are placed.

CHAPTER 4

THE ROYAL CITY

A visitor' to Copenhagen is reminded at many points that he is in a royal city. Above the capital S of the municipal railway stations there is a crown, also the gilded "pretzels" (a savoury pastry) at the doors of the bakeries show the crown. It does not necessarily follow that they are all "By Appointment of Her Majesty". Those who are, show this on their paper bags just as do the soda-water and beer producers on the labels of their bottles. The postmen will also remind you that they fulfil a regal duty, their jackets are of the same scarlet red as the royal guards. You will only see the guards in their gala uniform on special occasions.

A typical situation when the uniform used to be worn was on the late King Frederik IX's birthday when tens of thousands of Copenhagen citizens would flock to the square outside Amalienborg palace to present their best wishes. Many children were among this congratulating crowd, for there was no school on this day. The reception of the children was often a dialogue between the king and them. When he appeared on the balcony with his family everybody would cheer; as soon as he withdrew the children used to chant "Konge, Konge, kom nu frem, ellers gaar vi aldrig hjem" (King, King, come forward, otherwise we all will go home). After some time the king did re-appear, and one had the impression that he was hesitating and waiting to be asked to do so, not because he was arrogant, but because he obviously felt that the children enjoyed the chanting. And in Denmark you simply abide by what children like or dislike.

Also in the remainder of the city there was a distinctive birthday celebration atmosphere on the 11th of March, flags were flown everywhere, not just on public buildings. The "golden apples" danced on the water jets of the splendid Gammeltorv fountain as if they were table tennis balls at a fair-ground shooting gallery.

The scarlet gala of the royal guard also appeared, and still does appear, on a few other occasions: On the Queen Mother's birthday when a head of foreign state is met at the Central Station or when the Queen receives a new ambassador. On ordinary days the soldiers of the guard wear dark tunics with blue trousers. But even then, with their bearksins they look so much out of the ordinary that most visiting tourists take pictures of them or film them. Once upon a time the bearskins were designed to frighten the enemy and pursuade him to turn back, today this situation has been reversed; nonetheless the soldiers of the royal guard are the toughest of all the Danish army. The most opportune time to take photographs is at 12 noon, when the guards are changed at Amalienborg palace. Half an hour prior to this, the relieving unit marches off from the barracks adjoining Rosenborg palace, and pass through Gothersgade, Christian IX's Gade, Gammel Mønt, Østergade, Kongens Nytorv, Bregade, St. Annäplads, Amaliagade and finally arrive at the royal palace where the leaving sentries are already lined-up. Then, for 20 minutes, a ceremony is performed in that traditional style.

With the same punctuality as the soldiers the guided-tour coaches arrive at the site, you can take pictures and film as much as you like, ex-servicemen can pass a critical judgement as to the standards of the drill. Amalienborg is not only worth a visit because of the

The Stork Fountain.

bearskins, it also has a character and historic background of its own.

Strictly speaking the palace is not a single palace but is comprised of four which were built between 1749 and 1760 for some noble families. It was not until the fire at Christianborg palace in 1794 that Amalienborg became the royal residence.

One of the four buildings was the residence of the late King Frederik IX and his wife, Ingrid, the adjoining palace was occupied by the present Queen Margrethe and her husband Prince Henrik who is French-born and used to be Monsieur Henri. On the square is a well-known equestrian statue of King Frederik V by the French artist Saly; the monument was a gift from the East Asian Company, the biggest Danish enterprise. It was unveiled in 1770.

The Queen Mother comes from Sweden and is one of the few Swedes who speak an absolutely perfect Danish. Also the two younger daughters are married. Anne-Marie is the wife of the deposed King Constantine of Greece, whilst Benedikte married a German prince. The royal family has always been very popular. One of the reasons is certainly the fact that they join the people in their everyday life without any particular ceremony and fuss, which incidentally applies to other affluent Danish families.

There is another palace which was used by the royal family, namely Fredensborg by the main A6 road between Hillerød and Helsingør in North Zealand. Fredensborg palace was built under Frederik IV between 1719 and 1726. It takes its name from the peace treaty of 1720 which ended the great northern war. The present façade has classicist features. Many European monarchs visited Fredensborg, especially when Christian IX, "father-in-law of Europe" was in residence here. The park is laid-out in French style, patterned after Versailles. Seven alleyways run down to the nearby Lake Esrum, in the so called northern valley 60 sandstone figures represent farmers and fishermen from Norway, Iceland and the Färo Isles.

Another small palace in the northern outskirts of Copenhagen is Eremitagen in Dyrehave, "Deer Park" in

Klampenborg Forest. Eremitagen was built in 1736 by L. de Thura, commissioned by Christian VI, and still serves as a place of rest and refreshment for royal hunting parties. When the sun is shining, whether there is spring in the air or snow on the ground, and the Copenhagener wants a few hours in the country, the chances are he will go to Dyrehaven where thousands of these timid, graceful animals wander about at complete ease. A golf course, a summer fun-fair (open May 1 to August 15) and a number of all-year-round restaurants occupy the remainder of the 3500 acres of the forest area with paths and ponds, altogether an idyllic setting with magnificent views of the hills and the Sound.

Other palaces have long ceased to be used by the royal family. Within the city boundaries, in Østervoldgade, is Rosenborg set in the vast, pretty Kongens Have park. When Rosenborg was built under Christian IV from 1608 to 1617, it was outside the city and became the summer residence of the king. In 1833 it was transformed into a museum of the royal family. Renaissance-style Rosenborg contains not only a breathtaking display of all the Danish crown jewels but also a fine collection of furniture, together with the personal effects of Danish kings from the time of Christian IV, including the monarch's precious pearl-studded saddle. A more recent exhibit, King Frederik IX's fountain-pen with which he signed the revised constitution on 5th June, 1953, this was to enable the succession to the throne by the king's daughter since Frederik and Ingrid had no son. The priceless crown of Christian IV is also on display at Rosenborg, it is made of gold, enamel, pearls and hundreds of precious stones, it was made in Odense in 1596 and had a somewhat extraordinary fate: it had been pawned in Hamburg and was redeemed in 1648.

Another palace is to be found in Copenhagen, more precisely speaking in the borough of Frederiksberg, namely the Frederiksberg Palace which was begun under Frederik IV in 1699. Between 1708 and 1710 this building was extended by various annexes so that eventually it assumed the ground plan of an H, further extensions and arcades were added later on. The palace was modelled on the big Italian manor houses of this period. The vast park with its numerous canals must be seen as part of the entire estate. It was here that Frederik VI went boating with his family, today mothers take their children for a walk in the park which is open to the public, whilst the former palace accommodates a military academy.

Denmark's two most popular, and at the same time the two mightiest, castles are not in Copenhagen but some 30 miles from here in North Zealand, namely Frederiksborg and Kronbog castles.

The magnificent renaissance palace of Frederiksborg at Hillerød was built by Christian IV. It is completely surrounded by water. The construction work took 18 years, from 1602 to 1620. But the present buildings, except for the palace chapel, are of a much later date because in 1859 the castle was almost entirely gutted by fire.

It was restored by private subscriptions throughout the country and by money given by Carl Jacobsen, founder of the famous Carlesberg brewery.

Frederiskborg is now a national historic museum. A stroll through its halls and rooms is like a long walk through Danish history from the Vikings to the present.

An imposing watchpost at the entrance to Denmark, thus rises Kronborg Castle on the seashore of Helsingør, overlooking the narrowest passage of the Sound. As early as 800 years ago a castle stood on this site. The present Renaissance building dates back to 1574-1585. For centuries Kronborg was a thorn in the eyes of foreign sailors and merchants for it was here that the "Sound Dues" were collected from every ship entering or leaving the Baltic. These dues were in force for no less than 400 years, from 1429 to 1857. As you look at the walls of Kronborg another event will come alive, it was though an event which never took place here. It is also associated with a man who was never here either: Hamlet; it was here that he experienced the apparition of his father's ghost, and it was here that he spoke those famous Shakespearean words which have become immortal and are engraved on a plaque at the entrance gate.

For many years open-air Hamlet performances were staged in the courtyard of Kronborg castle during the summer. In the end the northern weather proved stronger, however, it is now being discussed whether or not to revive the Hamlet festivals. One can only hope that these efforts will be successful because a Hamlet performance at night in Kronborg castle has become an unforgettable experience to many people; great actors took the part of Hamlet here.

From 1725 until 1925 Kronborg was used as military barracks, since then it has been opened to visitors; the royal guards have an NCO training school in the castle which also houses a commercial and maritime museum, a relic of the military past are the dungeons where you will find the brooding figure of Holger the Dane who, according to the legend, will wake up and unsheathe his sword in Denmark's hour of danger. Holger Danske has however another place from where to strike, the statue in the dungeons of Kronborg is only a copy, the original is in the park of Marienlyst palace on the fringes of Helsingør. This palace was built as a sort of extension to Kronborg, and as a gift to widowed Queen Juliene Marie, from whom it takes its name. There are of course a number of other regal examples in Copenhagen, often the royal yacht "Danebrog" was moored in the harbour opposite the Customs Building, a slim white ship which did not look its age. The late king liked to steer the ship himself, he had a master's certificate. He used to sail on the yacht as far as Greenland, to the northern-most province of his realm.

We are also reminded of where we are by the large number of cars with the CD-badge at the rear which stands for Corps Diplomatique and means that these cars are exempt from tax and customs duty and their driver need not hold a driving licence. The CD-cars like the royal cars, are also allowed to enter Klampenborg Park which others may not.

There are 33 embassies and missions, 18 consulates in Copenhagen. Especially pretty in terms of architecture and setting are the British and French embassies, the former is in the 200 year-old Palais Lindencrone at St. Anna-Plads/corner Bregade. In front of the building is an equestrian statue of Christian X who lived through the German occupation from 1940 to 1945. As he is depicted on the monument he rode every morning through his capital, a few flowers in his hand which had been given to him by some child. The morning rides of their King became a symbol to the Danish people. At the next corner of St. Anna-Plads is another reminder of these days, a bust of US-president Franklin D. Roosevelt.

The American embassy is in a huge, modern block along a busy street, a building like many seen in other major cities of the world, immense and almost free from bacteria.

CHAPTER 5

THE OLD TOWN

Having been preoccupied with Copenhagen as a capital and Royal City it would seem reasonable for us to look into their past. In doing so, the first surprise is to find that the town in its early days was neither a capital nor royal. It was a modest fishermen's village from where a sort of ferry service was operated to the nearby island of Amager, or even right across the Sound to the opposite coast. The village had the simple name of Havn which means harbour, it was referred to by the Romans as 'Hafina', a name which continues to appear as trade and company names on many business premises and on the labels of canned food. From the start the people here combined prime production on the one hand, and services on the other hand, a typically Danish economic practice. A document dating back to 1043 mentions the village and trading place Havn. From archaeological finds we know, however, that in the town hall area farmers and fishermen must have lived much earlier. Flint stones have been found here which are six thousand years old.

Havn owes its first step from village to metropolis to Bishop Absalon. He was a martial character and is often depicted with a sword in his hand. In 1167 Absalon who was a foster-brother of the then ruling king as well as a powerful clergyman, built his first fortress on the site where the sixth Christiansborg stands today. Its ruins, a well and part of the prison tower, can be seen under the present building. Open from 10 a.m.-4 p.m. daily, with guided tours every hour.

Absalon became the founder of the city and 1167 became the year when Copenhagen was born. The monument of the bishop is at Højbroplads from where he has a good view across to Christiansborg. His helmet is a favourite rest place of seagulls, but only one at a time finds enough room to settle down.

Under the protective wings of Absalon and his successors who did not always see eye to eye with the kings, the city flourished and prospered. Protection was needed badly indeed in view of the north German rivals in commerce of those days. The young city is said to have been burned down at least twice by the Lübeck people.

A wall was added to the fortress, and merchants arrived in large numbers and settled. Soon one no longer simply referred to Havn (harbour) but to Købmandehavn (merchants' harbour) which eventually became København.

The quarrel between the bishops and the kings about the rule over the city lasted a long time approximately until the early 15th century. Up to that time you can easily identify the respective "master" of the state by whoever was in control of Copenhagen at a given time, the bishop or the king.

In 1417 this turbulent period once and for all came to an end; King Erik of Pommern placed Copenhagen under the rule of the crown, and the city became the king's residence and capital. The royal court, the fleet, garrison and suppliers by appointment of His Majesty, all moved to Copenhagen and in 1479 the university was founded.

Erik of Pommern wanted to make Copenhagen the "warehouse of the Baltic Sea". This again meant clashes and rivalry with the German merchants. Erik's successors

also showed their endeavour for, and concern about, the city. Their success in doing so, was varying.

Once, in 1536, the Copenhageners even had to endure a long siege, and had to surrender in the struggle for supremacy in the Baltic, but the city preserved its rights and then reformation came. More bad times befell the city in the 16th century. Between 1546 and 1583 the plague broke out no less than six times. Had this also been "imported" via Lübeck? Even today people in Denmark say to someone who looks pale and poorly "You look like the death from Lübeck".

The following century was at first a great era for Copenhagen, a sort of economic miracle. Christian IV whose reign was from 1588 to 1648, must have been very fond of his Copenhagen. He turned out to be the great architect and builder of the city. Everywhere you encounter his works, the design of which he took an active part. Christian built residential areas, palaces, business enterprises, cultural institutions, churches, students' homes, military installations and he laid-out a totally new city. We refer to Nybøder, near Østerport. Here Christian built 600 dwellings for the sailors of his navy. Today one would describe this as a company-owned housing scheme for skilled labour. The king did solve a labour market problem with this project. Before these houses were available, the king had to look for new sailors every spring because most of those from the previous year had vanished ashore during the winter. Now he offered the sailors decent homes in a good residential area, provided they were prepared to sign a contract for several years. With the hectic building construction work that Christian initiated everywhere, skilled labour must have been very much in demand.

The navy was given a new harbour: Christiansholm, also a church of their own: Holmen's Kirke. Also the Arsenal and the supply centre served military purposes. As for commerce, the Stock Exchange was built. The king did something special for education: Poor students were offered a home in which they could live free of charge and where they still do today: Regensen. The first legacy dwellings were destroyed by fire in 1728, the present ones date back to the 18th century.

The Round Tower emerged opposite Regensen. It was erected at the same time as the Trinity Church which originally had been intended as a students' church. An observatory was installed on the tower's platform. Since it would have been difficult to transport the heavy equipment over a narrow staircase the decision was made not to give the tower any stairs at all; instead a spiral ramp was built into the tower. It is more than 600 ft. long and the story goes that Czar Peter the Great of Russia rode up on horseback, and Czarin Catherine rode up in a horse-drawn carriage.

Opposite Slotsholmen, on the other side of the harbour on Amager island, Christian built an entirely new town Christianshavn, which first did not belong to Copenhagen at all. It was designed on Dutch examples. A canal cuts through the centre, parallel and at a right angle to it run the streets. The landside the town was shielded by heavy walls.

Our Saviour's Church with the spiral staircase winding around it on the outside, was added not until a later date: 1682-1692. It is the only Baroque-style church in Copenhagen.

Christian built the Rosenborg and Frederiksborg palaces for his own family. He even embarked on fashion designing; he created a horseman's armour which was much lighter than the knight's equivalent. His own armour measured 48 in. to the waist and only weighed 55 lbs.

All this happened at a time when the rest of Europe exerted itself in a thirty-year war. After this had been overcome Denmark also headed for stormy days. In 1658 it was defeated in a war with the Swedes and lost the provinces on the other side of the Sound, Scania, Halland and Blekinge. In 1659 the city itself was threatened by the Swedes who had marched across the ice of the Sound, but the city persevered and on the 11th February, 1659 the citizens of Copenhagen repulsed a large-scale attack by the Swedish army and thus spared their country the fate of Scania, Halland and Blekinge.

The King showed his gratitude to the Copenhageners by granting them new privileges. In some respect the citizens were given the same status as the nobility, in particular regarding payment of taxes and duties. The citizens could also now hold a public office and acquire land.

Fire, devestation and reconstruction, boom and prosperity, these were the characteristics of Copenhagen during the 18th and early 19th centuries. Catastrophies mark the features of Copenhagen which can still be seen in the old town.

In 1728 two fifths of the city were destroyed by a big fire, including 1670 houses, five churches, the town Hall and the University. More precautions were adopted during reconstruction work, and a number of thatched houses still standing at that time were replaced by more fire-resistant buildings. But this seemed to be of little effect for during the second big fire in 1795, a total of 941 houses were gutted by fire. Twelve years later from September 2nd to 4th, 1807, the city was shelled for three days and nights by a British landing force, a Hannoverian army corps under Wellington's command. This time 300 houses were destroyed and 1600 badly damaged and 1600 people lost their lives. After the Bombardment the British left taking with them the complete Danish fleet; the only vessel they left behind was a pleasure frigate which had once been a gift from the English King to his nephew, the Danish Crown-prince. There is a city map on which all of the districts affected by the three disasters are shown as shaded areas. Taken together they amount to almost the entire old town between town hall square and Kongens Nytorv. Only a few streets near Kongens Nytorv were spared.

This is why the old Copenhagen of today contains only very few buildings of mediaeval architecture. They are; the choir stalls of St. Peter's church which dates back to the early 15th century, the Holy Spirit House in Valkendorfsgade and the Senate building at the university, both of approximately the same period. The ruins of the tower at Jarmers Plads in Nørre Voldgade near the Town Hall Square is a remainder of the mediaeval fortifications. At this point Vandal chief Jarmer invaded and devestated the city in 1259. It was him after whom the Copenhageners have named this square, strange isn't it. Reconstruction work during the 19th century was carried out in a well-planned manner, though following the old pattern of the streets. Specified equal height of ridges, cornices and ledgements together with strictly observed alignment along the streets brought about a coherent overall townscape which makes old Copenhagen so attractive and brings back to reality an epoch which has long since gone by.

Already Christian IV had given the city a character of its own with his big Renaissance buildings. They were followed by those in Baroque architecture, of which the Charlottenborg Palace in Kongens Nytorv, now the Danish Academy of Fine Arts, Our Saviour's Church in Christianshavn and the Red Building in Slotsholmgade are particularly remarkable.

During the 18th century another era added much to Copenhagen's charm, it was the end of the Baroque period with it's German, French and Italian influence and the transition to Rococo. The most prominent architect of this time was N. Eigtved; he built the Marble Bridge on the south side of Christiansborg, the adjoining Crown-prince Palace, which today is the National Museum, and Amalienborg with the entire surrounding district. In this way a complete town district rose in Rococo style which is almost unique in the world.

This was made possible because of the ingenuity of a great architect sponsored by King Frederik V, both of whom we would describe as bold even by present-day standards. The King gave the building ground of Amalienborg and the surrounding land to families of the nobility on the condition that they would have their city residence built here according to Eigtved's plans. The new district was named Frederiksstad. The centre point became Frederik's statue mounted on horseback by Saly in the courtyard of Amalienborg Palace.

The Marble Church opposite Amalienborg was also part of the project. It was named Frederik's Church, but was not completed in its present form until the late 19th century.

The best method to cover old Copenhagen is to work your way through a bewildering jumble of winding streets and corners, and stroll through the area between the town hall square and Amalienborg.

The oldest major street which led from the western city gate to what is today the town hall square, was Vestergade; it's slightly wavy pattern seems to follow the tracks of horse-drawn carriages which may have determined the route of this access road. Through Vestergade you soon arrive at the city's oldest square, namely Gammel Torv (Old Market) with the city's oldest fountain. The southern half of this double square is called Nytorv (New Market). The old town hall which stands at Nytorv houses today the Court of Justice. As you stroll in a northerly direction from Gammeltorv you find yourself in front of tow churches: the cathedral with Thorvaldsen's Christ and Apostles, and St. Peter's Church; at the same time you can see the University.

There used to be a town hall opposite the cathedral, at the entrance to Studiesträde, then it became the site for the first University. Since the reformation it has been the residence of the bishops and the monument on the small square is in commemoration of the reformation.

When you walk from St. Peter's church through the passage between the cathedral and the university, and cross Frue Plads you arrive at Fiolsträde, which is Copenhagen's second "pedestrians only" zone. The decision to declare this street a pedestrian zone was taken following the successful earlier experiment with Strøget which is also the longest of its kind in Europe, over a mile long.

In Fiolsträde you will find some interesting bookshops, after all we are near the university.

If you bear left in a southerly direction from Gammel-torv you will soon stand by the canal in Nybrogade and Gammel Strand opposite Slotsholmen, where lobsters and crabs in the spotlessly clean basement windows of the fishmongers prove a mouthwatering sight to the tourists. During the mornings you can still see a few fisherwomen sitting infront of the Højbro Plads opposite Christiansborg at the end of the Gammel Strand. They are the last of a whole guild of fishwives who for many years dominated the scene on this site. They have in the meantime been moved to the more modern market in the outskirts of the city, much to the regret of many amateur photographers. Only a few were allowed to stay, but a monument was erected on this site, showing fisherwoman Hanne who once was very active here. If you want to explore this part of the city, you have to comb through the whole area between Fiolsträde and the canal. Allow yourself some time for the small basement shops with their crates infront of the doors containing old books, cans and jugs, pokers and porcelain figures. You can also do endless window shopping here for pipes, toys, decent and less decent books, genuine and fake souvenirs. The old facades with brightly-coloured advertisements, the bars with juke boxes, the small gourmet restaurants, the expensive shops in Strøget, the rest benches in open-air, the sausage stalls, also of course for Helligaand's Church, Grabrødre Torv (the market of the Grey Brothers), are all worth seeing. The mayonnaise district, so called by the Copenhageners because its streets bear such deliciously sounding names as Salmon or Lobster Street, the fruit and flower market at Højbro Plads with the Storch Fountain, a gift from the Danish midwives and more recently the meeting point of genuine and would-be hippies should not be missed.

On these winding paths you will automatically include some of Christian IV's works, the Round Tower and the Regensen, are in the midst of this area.

At the end of Strøget the street widens into Østergade which joins Copenhagen's largest square, Kongens Nytorv. On your left you see Denmark's most expensive hotel, the "d'Angleterre", on the opposite side to the right is the Royal Theatre and the Charlottenborg, and at the centre is a mounted statue of Christian V. Near the end of June every year, newly graduated students arrive here in horse-drawn wagonettes and dance gaily around the silent figure of the king.

Before you arrive at Amalienborg on your way from Kongens Nytorv you cross another quaint area; the stretch of water running from Kongens Nytorv to the harbour, this is the Nyhavn Canal. Picturesque 18th century buildings, most of them containing sailors' cafés, are crammed in along the left side whilst the right-hand side is devoted to more serious work. On the left-hand side the houses are colourful as are the "establishments" and the hoardings for dancing and tattooing. Incidentally, the police cover their beat here in twos!

At the entrance to Hyhavn there is a huge anchor to commemorate Danish sailors who lost their lives during the last war.

On both sides at the end of Nyhavn are the quays for passenger liners, the one on the left for the routes to Jutland and Norway, on the right for the Sound ferry service and the boats to Bornholm island.

If you go down Bregade, which is one of the most exquisite office-block and shopping streets, and take the first turning to the right which goes to Sankt Annae Plads, then the next left into Amaliegade through an imposing colonnade, you will finally arrive infront of the four royal palaces.

CHAPTER 6

MODERN COPENHAGEN

Fortified walls were turned into parks — The city grows and bursts at the seams — The first high-rise apartment houses — City of the future on Amager Island. During the 19th century the city grew into the modern era. But the new century had at first nothing good install for the city. In 1807 the British had bombarded Copenhagen, in 1814 Norway was separated from the Danish realm by the treaty of Kiel, Copenhagen was described in a contemporary report as a "plucked" city in an impoverished country. The fleet had shrunk, many companies collapsed and Hamburg became the leading merchant and finance metropolis of northern Europe.

But then the steam ship arrived and in 1847 Copenhagen had it's first railway link to Roskilde.

In 1840 the population of the city totalled 120,000. A new constitution was introduced and a new enlarged council could now be elected directly by the citizens, but only 2000 Copenhageners made use of their electoral rights.

In 1860 the first underground sewage system was built and in 1870 the great industrial boom began.

In terms of architecture the city was now under the influence of Neo-classicism. A new Christiansborg and also a new Town Hall were built, the latter today housing the court of justice at Nytorv, then the cathedral, the Metropolitan School and a foundation at No. 34, Skindergade. All these are works by C.F. Hansen who was also a famous architect in north Germany.

Bindesbøll built Thorvaldsen's Museum, in 1857 Amagerport, Vesterport and Øserport, all part of the former fortifications, were demolished and replaced in 1872 by vast parks for the public.

In the following years the Langelinie promenade was laid-out by the harbour, together with the free port. During this time the Marble Church was completed, and the Royal Theatre was moved to the new big building at Kongens Nytorv, and the Pantomime Theatre was opened in the Tivoli Gardens.

Soon the city grew beyond the old boundaries, Vesterbro and Nørrebro became the new residential areas with grey streets, old-style apartment houses and backyards which but a few decades later are to be declared development areas. In 1911 the population of Copenhagen was 462,000 and together with Frederiksberg and Gentofte, the total was 700,000.

After the first World War new housing estates emerged from a concept which even today continues to be adopted as the new course: The people of the city shall live in an environment of sunshine and parkland. The architects Ivar Bentsen and Thorkild Henningsen built the first modern rows of houses set amidst communal parks. Large-scale housing estates were to follow with dwellings of various types with lots of flower-bright balconies and recreation areas for children and adults. One of these districts is in Bispebjerg in the north of the city. In 1921 the foundation stone was laid for Grundtvig's Church on Bispebjerg, Copenhagen's highest site, 100 ft. above sea level. The church which was consecrated in 1940 and stands in memory of N.S.F. Grundtvig, clergyman, poet, and founder of Denmark's adult education system. The funds for the building were raised

The famous Tivoli Gardens.

by a nationwide collection. Eight bricklayers and artisans toiled nineteen years to build this church, using over five million bricks all of Danish origin. Grundtvig's church has an organ-pipe facade in the style of a typical Danish village church. Many of the apartment blocks on Bispebjerg which were built during the same period can compete with latest "new towns" of other European cities; this applies also to Vestersøhus which overlooks the lakes near downtown Copenhagen. In the suburbs new residential areas grew fast with many small detached houses surrounded by lovely gardens; surprisingly they are not villas for wealthy people, but healthy dwellings for working-class families.

After 1945 the shortage of housing became particularly acute. The city grew and grew, Copenhagen became Greater Copenhagen with all the independent boroughs surrounding it. In most cases complete new satelite towns surrounding a centralised heating plant were planned.

The shortage of housing added new features to the city's skyline, in the early fifties the first "skyscrapers" rose in Bellahøj next to the big field on which Denmark's most popular country show is held every summer. From the balconies of the high-rising blocks in Bellahøj you have a view over the entire city and as far as the Swedish coast.

The most recent Copenhagen developments are in the west, where new satelite towns have grown up in Rodovre, Glostrup, Taastrup and Gladsaxe, with colossal apartment blocks, shopping streets and centres.

Where else could Copenhagen expand? It was the military forces who helped solve this difficult problem which exists all over the world. Military training ground to the west of Amager was released for development purposes. Its boundaries are only ¾ mile from the city centre, the whole area is as big as the present inner Copenhagen district.

Vestamager as this new town of the future for 120,000 people is called, has already been completed as far as the drawing board. A large-scale competition among designers and architects produced revolutionary conceptions for the Copenhagen City of the year 2000.

According to them, by the end of this century, Copen-hageners will live in atrium houses, garden houses, terrace dwellings and apartment blocks, traffic, amenities and car-parks will be accommodated in a multi-level network. Vestamager, according to Lord Mayor Urban Hansen, can be visualised as the Export Supermarket for the whole of northern Europe, especially once you can go to, and come from, Sweden in a few minutes over a bridge starting at Amager.

The Copenhageners are very keen on their parks, this one is the King's Park.

CHAPTER 7

THE GREEN CITY

The Copenhageners like to be surrounded by something green and since this is not always possible in open air they provide substitutes within their own homes, where you find a multitude of plants and shrubs; they are labelled with the most fantastic names such as "Mother-in-law's Gossip" or "King's Wine". Plenty of open-air parks have also been provided right in the city. Where the old fortifications and walls once ran along Nørre Voldgade and Øster Voldgade, today you will find H.-C. Ørstedspark, the Botanic Gardens and Østre Anläg which continue towards the harbour via the Citadel and finally the Langelinie.

In this way you can walk around the entire old town on almost uninterrupted grass or to put it another way: From any point of central Copenhagen, you can within a matter of minutes be in open parkland, where you can feed swans, ducks, pigeons, sparrows or even yourself. Also, even within the city centre every little space available is utilised and beautified by something green, a few immense flower pots and seat benches. If there is no bench seat nearby, maybe there is a fountain, or a high kerbstone on which you can rest without hesitation. There are vast green areas, in the outer districts, Sønder-marken and Frederiksberg Have are huge green spots west of the city, also Fälledparken in the north. You can walk in an outer ring through parks from the northern fringes of the city to the outskirts of Øre Sound near Valby. This is not a ringroad but rather a ring-path or cycle track. We should mention that this trip is not a simple walk but more a hiking tour.

In recent years additional recreation areas have been created although the new housing estates are already set amidst greens. Utterslev Mose in the north became the major green belt and national park of the city.

To the citizens of the city each of these green dots on the map assumes a specific function. The parks along the old fortifications are for a rest from the hectic life in the city centre, Frederiksberg Have and the Zoo mean that at long last you can see the polar bears and bison which come from the domestic province of Greenland. You can also watch the monkeys and apes, which look at times, so human. Copenhagen's Zoo is more than a hundred years old and one of the biggest in Europe. It contains 2500 animals of 800 different species and 700 birds of 500 different varieties.

Langelinie is not only for the foreign visitors. Here, the inhabitants not only show the visitors, but also their children, the Little Mermaid. The graceful bronze figure perched on a rock who drinks in the sea with pensive eyes. Created by the sculptor Edvard Eriksen, the model was a ballerina of the royal ballet. She became one of the most photographed ladies in the world; the model only died a few years ago. The saying is that the artist was the model's lover, and that he followed the lines of her body, but for the head used his wife as a model. A few years ago, someone cut-off the mermaid's head one night, but a new one was soon cast and the attempt by the unknown person, to make money by selling the story unfortunately misfired.

Langelinie means to simply stroll along by the foreign navy vessels and big ocean liners moored here every summer. It can also mean simply to park your car for a while on the quayside during daytime or by night and gaze across the sea to the industrialised side of the harbour and the old fortress Tre Kroner at the harbour entrance.

When you enter Langelinie walking from Amalienborg you arrive first at the Gefion Fountain, a mighty legend in bronze and water of the goddess Gefion and four oxen who were in fact her sons. The myth tells us that Gefion converted the young men into oxen when she was promised that she could keep as much land as she was able to plow round in a day. Gefion's trick proved rather profitable. The sons turned out to be a powerful team and plowed the whole of Zealand, Copenhagen's main island out of Sweden. The hole thus left in Sweden became Lake Värner. And when you look at the map you can see that the legend is true, Lake Värner and Zealand show almost matching contours.

Something entirely different to the Copenhageners is Fälledparken, the big public park. To them it means demonstrations with fun and leisure at the same time. Why not, after all they need not be excluded from one another. For many years Fälledparken has been the big rally ground. On the 1st of May a big public entertainment takes place here. Every Sunday at 4 p.m. there is a concert by a seventy-piece orchestra. The vast green area is for everyone, old and young Copenhageners alike lie in the grass for picnics, with their families. They do whatever is conducive to their recreation, play soccer or watch others as they exert themselves. Grass to the Copenhagener is not a sacred "out-of-bounds" area, he may sit or lie in the sunshine as and when he feels like it even if it is only for a few minutes during lunch break.

Open-air concerts not only take place in Fälledparken, but also in the Frederiksberg park infront of the palace a concert is given once a week, and occasionally in Strandpark on Amager Island.

*Outdoor theatre
in the
Tivoli Gardens.*

CITY OF ENTERTAINMENT,
CULTURE AND EDUCATION

The most famous park in Copenhagen is Tivoli Gardens, a chapter of its own. Tivoli is a 20 acres amusement park between the Central Railway Station and the Town Hall. Originally the ground was to serve military purposes as a fortress. Fortunately George Carstensen, a Danish architect and literalist, had the idea to take out a lease for the area outside the city walls. He formed "Copenhagen Summer Tivoli Limited" and on August 15, 1843 the amusement park was opened.

Tivoli is neither Vienna's Prater nor the Bois de Boulogne nor Battersea Park which was, incidentally, modelled on the Copenhagen forerunner, Tivoli is Copenhagen.

Tivoli has a timetable of its own with a greatly varying curriculum. Lessons are for young and old in the art to live and let live.

Tivoli is open from May to September, during the winter it becomes a car park. The gates open at 9 a.m. Then comes the time during which almost 30 restaurants from the luxurious establishment to the self-service recess where you can unwrap your own sandwiches, the kiosks, stalls, are supplied with whatever vitals the visitors might ask for. Cars coast slowly through the park, beer wagons are drawn by heavy brewery horses, sun hats on their ears and colourful ribbons on their harness.

To the visitor without official business Tivoli is a place of rest during these morning hours. Between the huge flower beds are bench seats, ducks swim across the pond, and everyone is free to decide whether he wants to read a newspaper, do some knitting, brood and contemplate, or feed the ducks. If you are a young couple you can hold hands without interference from a third party.

Towards noon the second lesson begins. The hour of the Danish breakfast approaches. Maybe someone is invited by a friend to one of the posh and somewhat pricy restaurants where that astonishing institution known as "cold buffet" holds sway at lunch time. This consists of an enormous table groaning with an assortment of fish and cold game followed by a hot dish and ending with cheese, Schnaps, coffee and brandy. The father who has to look after a large family will presumably prefer one of those establishments where Smørrebrød is available in large numbers and wide varieties. This is accompanied by beer for mummy and daddy, for the children, lemonade in all colours and shades.

At 2 p.m. the amusement stands, galleries etc. open, the merry-go-rounds and the ferris wheel begin to emit their doodle music, from the big dipper come the first screams and the minitrain rolls on rubber wheels through the park. Then come the afternoon concerts and with them the coffee time of ladies' parties.

Towards the evening Tivoli gathers momentum to turn into a great show. The Pantomime Theatre begins its' performances, the orchestras and bands play without interfering with each other, some of them light, others more sedate music. There are ten permanently engaged orchestras at Tivoli, the biggest of which plays in the New Concert Hall which seats 2000. During a season there are 12 symphonic concerts often with world-famous conductors and solists.

On Plänen, the big open-air stage at the centre of the gardens, leading stars of variety shows perform, Josephine Baker and other famous singers have performed here. Somebody who is engaged to appear at the Tivoli belongs to international top class.

In the narrow passageway behind the Slide, people crowd in front of one-arm bandits, a panopticum and a mice theatre. All sorts of other entertainment and fun roll on ceaselessly, the man with the scissors cuts one silhouette after another of people's heads, the soft-ice taps never stand still, and time and again chairs and seats tempt you to rest and enjoy the golden Danish beer.

On Saturdays and Sundays the Tivoli Guard marches through the gardens, a group of toytown soldiers dressed in the style of the Royal Guard, aged between 10 and 16.

Three times a week, Wednesday, Saturday and Sunday, the Tivoli Day ends with a Firework Display before midnight.

Tivoli Gardens are visited every season by between four to five million people and astonishing it may sound it is nonetheless true that a number among them continue to be Copenhageners so that Tivoli remains what its founder wanted it to be "Copenhagen Summer Tivoli".

If you want to watch the Copenhageners at leisure among themselves you have to go to Bakken.

Bakken means hill or hillock and lies in the oak woods of Klampenborg on the northern outskirts of the city. A public fun fair which is somewhat less refined than Tivoli, more rusticated and also louder, is held on Bakken from April to August. Here people sing, drink and play, the slide is higher than the one at Tivoli, it is the longest in Europe. Marquees with brass bands and beer taps bear household names like "Zillertal" "Sangglade Naverhule". There are bowling alleys and bingo halls, striptease and harlequins, the latter addressing their audience with the formula: "Welcome children and all of you who were children and those who are still looking forward to becoming children." Famous Danish artists appear at Brakken, among them one of the tallest and greatest comedians in the country, Dirch Passer.

As you emerge from Bakken you find yourself immediately in a most beautiful oak-tree forest. The S-line
station Klampenborg on the other hand is no further
than a few hundred yards away. When you walk in the
opposite direction deeper into the forest you will arrive
at Dyrehaven with its numerous deer, quiet paths and
enormous trees.

If you do not feel like a long walk through the woods
you can hire a horse-drawn carriage and cross the vast
park which belongs to the Queen as you can see from
the coat of arms above the high wooden entrance gates.
Entertainment and culture in Copenhagen do not only
exist in open-air you have also a choice of theatres and
museums.

The city contains seventy museums some of which
command world-wide reputation, others don't and yet
even in these you feel like wrapping-up one or two
objects.

Those who know Copenhagen and remember its museums
are as a rule prompted to think of beer and brewery, a
notion which in Copenhagen is not necessarily original
in this context because beer can come to mind here at
many other places as well.

But in the case of museums this has a special bearing
because where would Copenhagens museums be without
the brewery boss Carl Jacobsen and without the
Carslberg breweries. To them the city owes its most
famous museum, the Glyptotek, precisely speaking the
New Carlsberg Glyptotek. Jacobsen founded it in 1882,
subsequently made it a gift to the municipality together
with a "relative foundation". The relative foundation
was the profit of his breweries. If and when you drink
beer in Copenhagen you thereby have an opportunity
of doing something for culture and art.

This incidentally applies not only to Carlsberg, but also
to Tuborg, the other big brewery which has merged with
Carlsberg and frequently makes donations for cultural
and scientific causes.

Also the restoration of the Frederiksborg Palace at
Hillerød and the foundation of the National History
Museum are associated with the name of Carl Jacobsen.

His villa on the brewery premises is residence of honour for a famous Danish scientist of today. Niels Bohr lived here and after his death the archaeologist Professor Johannes Brødsted moved in.

Carl Jacobsen who died in 1914 did a lot more for his native town. Even within his business he did something for the arts in the style of his time, as is reflected by the ornamental gates, buildings and towers on the brewery premises. In 1879 he initiated the "Albertina Foundation" the interest yields of which were to be used for improvement and beautification of public squares and parks, the bronze mermaid by Langelinie was a personal gift by him. He even had a spire placed upon the Nikolaj Church and the Jesus Church was also commissioned by him. In 1902 he made his entire brewery business a gift to the Carlsberg Trust on the condition that the returns therefrom should form the basis of the simultaneously initiated Ny Carlsberg Foundation. The latter not only maintains the Glyptotek but also subsidises arts and artists in Denmark by purchasing works of arts which are intended for public buildings in the provinces, parks, sports grounds and schools, wherever people meet and gather.

The Glyptotek contains reputable collections including ancient Greek works which are associated with the archaeologist Dr. Frederik Poulsen. The museum houses Roman statuary, the gallery contains world famous paintings by the great impressionists as well as modern works. An ancient column, stands infront of the museum a gift from the city of Rome. The Beatrice statue on its top is a work by the Danish sculptor Utzon-Frank.

The National Museum is the largest museum in northern Europe and also has a world-wide reputation. It contains Danish prehistoric and historic collections, amongst others the 2500 - 3000 years old Sun Chariot and the Hindsgavl Dagger, fashioned and used several thousand years before the birth of Christ. Furthermore you can get some idea of Viking camp life and the ships in which they sailed all over the world. Another fascinating asset of the museum are the oldest ethnographical collections in the world including Eskimos, Indians, Asians, also a comprehensive coin collection. The galleries of the museum cover almost 2 miles.

Many Danes have contributed towards the wealth of the museum. They went out as amateur archaeologists and sent many of their finds to the National Museum. Other departments of the National Museum are the Museum of Denmark's Struggle for Freedom between 1940 and 1945 housed in Esplanaden near Langelinie, and an open air museum "Frilandmuseet" near Lyngby.

The National Art Gallery "Statens Museum for Kunst" is housed in a big building in Øster Voldgade. Its collections of paintings, sculptures and replicas are so extensive that the big building has long become too small, and has had to be modified. Nearby, in Stockholmsgade, is the Hischsprung Collection of 1902 with paintings, drawings and sculptures by Danish artists of the 19th century. It is a gift by cigar manufacturer Hirschsprung.

Rosenborg Palace, also in Øster Voldgade, is the museum of the royal family.

Another art gallery is a gift by a barrister and supreme court QC, C.L. David. The David Collection at No. 30, Kronprinzessengade, contains Oriental and European handicraft and paintings by foreign masters.

The latest Art Collection which has made the headlines outside Denmark, was the gift of the owner of a cheese factory. Louisiana is a collection of modern art. At Louisiana which is set by the cliffs of a magnificent bay on the Sound near Humlebäk there are also frequent exhibitions of modern art from all over the world. Louisiana is not intended to attract only the experts, it is also designed for family outings. There is a vast green in the park where you can stretch out and have a rest, in a self-service cafe you can unwrap your own sandwiches and there is a special room for children where they can try-out their own artistic talents on the walls with numerous brushes and lots of paint. The entrance door is so small that adults have to bend down to get through. In this way there is never a crowd of adults inside, after all the room is for the children. Louisiana, the former stately home, takes its name from its first occupant who had been married in succession to three women all with the first name of Louise.

Thorvaldsen's Museum also belongs to the city of

Copenhagen, as does the City Museum in Vesterbro, in the latter there is an account of the city's history and the life of its citizens in former times. Here you can see relics of famous Copenhageners such as Holberg and H.C. Andersen. A separate department is devoted to Søren Kierkegaard whose grave is at the Assistenz cemetery. The Museum of Decorative Art (Kunstindustrimuseet) is at No. 68, Bredgade; the building was formerly a hospital and forms part of the Rococo district around Amalienborg. The museum contains handicraft from the Middle Ages to the present day. Also in the same building is the Musical History Museum with two thousand musical instruments, paintings and books.

In the former Court Theatre in the south wing of Christianborg Palace is the Theatrical History Museum which contains personal effects and portraits from the time of Holberg (1684-1754) to the present day.

Also the Royal Danish Arms Museum is accommodated on a historic site in the old Arsenal building on Slotsholmen island.

There are further museums in the outskirts; Amager Museum is accommodated in an old half-timbered farmhouse in the village of Store Magleby in the south of Amager island. It is an account of the island's cultural history and how Christian II settled the Dutch peasants during the 16th century to supply his court with vegetables.

Dragør Museum on Amager island describes the way of life and costumes of the island's first inhabitants who had arrived from Holland in 1521. Dragør as a whole has retained its features as a farming and fishing village. Totalling only 57 houses, this quaint old village is under a preservation order. The museum is in the village's oldest house by the harbour.

The most important out-of-town museum is the open air "Frilandsmuseet" near Sorgenfri in the north of Copenhagen. In a park covering 40 acres there is a collection of reconstructed old Danish farms, several windmills and country houses moved here from other parts of Denmark and south Sweden. The houses are completely furnished and equipped with the implements and utensils of the respective period and area to which they belong. Across the street is the Agricultural Museum.

On the farms of Frilandsmuseet you can witness practical work being carried out from May to September, work to the benefit of the visitor so that he can form a realistic view of what sort of activities took place in this part of the country in the old days: embroidery, weaving, amber-cutting, then there is a pottery and a water-operated mill. During the weekend there is a display of folkdancing and in May you can watch the shearing of the sheep. You can move about the whole vast area in a horse-drawn carriage.

In Charlottenlund, near the Øre Sound, is the Fisheries Museum, a small house with a charm of its own. Here you can see the results of Danish deep-sea research fishing gear of earlier and present times is on display and you learn what the food of the future, seaweed and plankton, looks like. All sorts of strange fish are exhibited, for instance the largest haddock ever caught in Danish waters and fish with malformations, such as a cod with the head of a cat.

If you want to see living fish of all descriptions and origin you can do so in the Danish Aquarium opposite the Fisheries Museum. Sharks, eals and exotic fish, roam in huge basins, there are also the dangerous piranhas which can strip a cow or any other mammal to the bones in a matter of minutes. Not far from Charlottenlund is the Ordrupgaard, a stately home with collections of Danish handicraft, furniture and paintings, including some 19th century French impressionists.

The Museum of Trade and Shipping is in Kronborg Castle near Helsingør; it contains exhibits relating to Denmark's maritime history and trade also of the former colonies in the West Indies.

The Hunting and Forestry Museum is at Hørsholm. It is the only one of its kind and size in Europe, containing collections of hunting gear and arms from early and recent times, plants and all animals which could be, and still can be, hunted in Denmark.

The Viking Ships at Roskilde are one of the latest exhibitions; these ships were found, salvaged and thoroughly restored only a few years ago. The museum is interesting under various aspects; you get some idea of what formidable fellows the Vikings must have been when you see the ships and realise how far they sailed in them across the oceans. One has an insight into their art of shipbuilding for even today, boats continue to be assembled by Viking methods. At the same time the museum is a workshop where you can watch restoration work being carried out, and finally the complex is quite a sight from an architectural point of view with its high glazed facade immediately by the Fjord banks.

When the word theatre is mentioned, the foreign visitor to Copenhagen immediately thinks of the Royal Theatre, "Det Kongelige Teater", known by the locals as "Det Kongelige". The first royal stage opened in 1748 and later became the Royal Theatre maintained by the government. Preceding these early royal ventures, there was another theatre in Lille Grønnegade for which Ludvig Holberg wrote comedy plays.

The building of the Royal Theatre at Kongens Nytorv dates back to 1874. Performances run from 1st September to 31st May on two stages, the "old" and the "new" stage. The latter is actually an annexe to the old Theatre building and because of its elevated position is colloquially referred to as the "Starling Box". The programme features drama, opera and ballet. The Ballet has a world-wide reputation; August Bournonville who was the chief choreographer of the Royal Theatre from 1830 to 1877, laid the foundation stone of this reputation. His style and approach continue even today to be the fundamentals of the teaching at the Royal Ballet School which is attached to the Theatre. Children are admitted to this school at the early age of seven to eight.

The season ends each spring with a Ballet Festival which lasts a whole week and is rated as a great event on the international ballet scene.

The regular ballet performances during the season also attracts foreign visitors and many ballet enthusiasts travel from all over Europe to see the Royal Ballet.

In terms of drama Det Ny Teater must be rated equal to the Royal Theatre. This new private theatre in

Vesterbrogade dates back to 1908. Leading Danish artists perform here and the season runs from August to June.

The Folk Theatre "Folketeatret" in Nørregade has a fairly regular audience, it's season is also from August to June; it is more than a hundred years old.

A more recent theatre is Fiol-Teatret, a small stage at No. 9, Halmtorvet, near the Central Railway Station, which soon established a reputation of its own; it is in the modern style of the so called cellar theatres, or "fringes", and is open from August to May. ABC-Teatret is Denmark's only and very charming Revue Theatre; the comedy presented at ABC-Theatre is not the sledge-hammer type, more the sort of humour where one does not take oneself too seriously and still can laught at oneself. Open all year round.

Other theatres are: Der Ny Scala, Ungdommens Teater and Gladsaxe Teater. The most reputed orchestra of Copenhagen is the Royal Theatre's Orchestra "Det Kongelige Kapel" with 100 musicians some of whom also perform chamber music. For 300 years the orchestra has been rated top-level throughout Europe, which means world-wide reputation. Apart from its function as the orchestra of the royal theatre, they also perform a number of separate concerts every year.

The second outstanding orchestra in Copenhagen is the Radio Symphony Orchestra which is often under the direction of famous foreign conductors. The 50 radio concerts given a year, of which 20 are the so called "Thursday Concerts", are open to the public and admission here is less than for other concerts. Even less expensive are the Sunday Concerts performed every Sunday during the winter.

During the summer Copenhagen's musical life takes place in the Tivoli Gardens. The Tivoli Symphony Orchestra plays every evening, often with foreign soloists, admission free. Once a week there is a symphony concert for which you have to pay, tickets are not always easily available.

As for the smaller Copenhagen orchestras, we must mention "Collegium Musicum" which is largely formed by the musicians of the Royal Theatre Orchestra and performs in the Glyptotek. Det Unge Tonkunstnerskab, the young musicians' association, formed in 1920, is devoted to modern music to the extreme, they give 20 concerts during the winter most of them in museums.

Amalienborg Palace with the port in the background.

CHAPTER 9

ECONOMY AND HARBOUR

Copenhagen is an economically minded city and welcomes tourists for very realistic reasons as well as pleasurable ones. But there are much more powerful resources to keep Copenhagen alive.

In terms of economy and industry Copenhagen covers also all the surrounding boroughs which together form Greater Copenhagen. This area stretches from Køge Bay in the south, to north Zealand a distance of 50 miles. Also to the west, towards Roskilde, the city is expanding at a fast rate. It is here where the most advanced satelite towns are rising. New industrial estates have been developed out of town because Copenhagen has long become too small for industry. In Copenhagen itself a quite special solution was devised to solve the problem. An area of many hundred acres in the shallow water of Øre Sound was surrounded by dykes, and the land reclaimed. In this way building ground for 150 new factories was provided, which will offer jobs to 20,000 people. It may not be easy to find the labour, but on the other hand the metropolis attracts people from the countryside because hourly wages here are 2 Kr. higher.

Copenhagen's largest industrial company is Burmeister & Wain, engineering plant and shipbuilding yards, which make an impressive background as they loom across the harbour when you take a picture of the little mermaid by Langelinie. B&W have 10,000 employees the company became famous with its Diesel engines for marine purposes. They were the first in the world. The first vessel without a funnel was MS "Selandia" of the "Østasiatisk Kompanie" which sailed on its maiden voyage from Langelinie in 1912.

Today almost one third of all the ships in the world are equipped with B&W engines which were either built in Copenhagen or under licence throughout the world.

Other Copenhagen companies turn out specialised products which have also won world-wide reputation, installations for cement factories and beer, for instance. The two leading breweries have an output of 180 Million pints a year. Such quantities cannot of course be consumed in Denmark or on Danish ships alone. Danish beer is sold all over the world even to the canteen of the United Nations in New York.

The Royal Porcelain Manufacture and Bing & Grøndahl supply the world with Copenhagen chinaware. The same applies to Gerog Jensen in the field of silverware. At the top of Copenhagen's industry is metalworking industry followed by foodstruffs. Who hasn't heard of Danish canned food?

In a city which owes its foundation and development to it's harbour, and which continues to depend on the harbour as it's vital backbone, it is obvious that trade and services play an important part. The only stock exchange of the country is in Copenhagen and so is the only free harbour. The largest trading company in Denmark is OK (Østasiatisk Kompanie) with a turnover totalling thousands of millions. ØK has plantations and nurseries of their own overseas, a merchant fleet of their own and business interests all over the world. The most important private shipowner of the world was also a Copenhagener: A.P. Møller. His company "Märsk" which is now managed by his son, owns ships totalling 1.6 Million tons unladen weight. This is also the only company that holds a licence to bore for oil and gas in the soil of Denmark.

Services is something for which the Danes have a natural talent. Their Banks are large and modern, nobody shows any surprise when a guest in a pub or restaurant pays his bill by cheque. Even the so called ordinary man know how to handle and manage a cheque book.

Many government authorities and private companies have their offices cleaned by Danish Office Cleaning Company which operate their crews via radio and which in the meantime has opened branches in a number of other countries, employing a total of almost 20,000 people.

All this industry started some six thousand years ago when a man opened a flint stone workshop near Gammel Torv. Maybe he even placed a stone infront of the entrance to his cave with an inscription that today would read like this "Jenesen's flint stones are the best in the world, they are Danish".

Copenhagen's oldest, still existing industrial plant is Kongens Bryghus (Royal Brewery) which despite its proud name today only produces beer for children, nannies, drivers and teatotallers.

An industrial boom took place in the city during the 17th and 18th centuries when businessmen from Germany and Holland built tobacco curing houses, sugar refineries, soap factories and silk-weaving mills. The technological evolution in the past century is reflected in the streets of Vesterbro and Nørrebro with their grey, monotonous houses contrasting with the "posh" residential areas of Frederiksberg and Hellerup which came about during the same period.

Despite wide-spread industry, the city has always remained a Harbour in the mind of its' people. Obvious features are the seagulls that populate the tops of chimneys, lantern masts and monuments, the atmosphere that carries a taste of salt, and the smell of seawater, oil and tar. This mixture of smells is most pronounced in Kalvebodderne, Havnegade, Kvästhusbroen and as far out as Langelinie, in which case you have at the same time completed a walk around the harbour. It begins at the bulkgoods docks at Kalvebod Brygge with the Islands Brygge in the background. Mixed cargo is handled at the long quays and ramps of Christiangade on Slotsholmen island. The passenger terminal area begins at Knippelbro, this side for the services to Bornholm and Sweden, on the other side to Iceland and Färo isles. The terminal for the Hydrofoils, which cross the Sound to Malmø in Sweden within 35 minutes, is at the end of the Hyhavn and on the other side at the entrance to Christianshavn the boats to Greenland are moored.

The Skt. Annäplads and Amalienborg quays belong to the ships of Jutland and Norway. Further north is the Customs administration and then the Langelinie begins at Gefion Fountain the "green" part of the harbour with the big modern pavilion of the Royal Yachting Club and the luxurious yachts in the sailboat harbour. At the end of the long quay where the naval vessels moor when visiting Copenhagen, you get a glimpse of the Free Harbour.

The Free Harbour was laid-out in 1894 when the Copenhageners feared that the new canal linking the North Sea and the Baltic, might give Hamburg an excessive advantage. The name Hamburg has up to now not lost a certain worrying effect; a watchful eye is constantly directed towards Hamburg, more recently its an even more watchful eye as a new Hamburg airport is to be built at Kaltenkirchen which might prove an unwelcome rival to their own new airport project at Saltholm.

The new big airport of the north is to be built on Saltholm island in the sound between Denmark and Sweden, the island belongs to Denmark. Copenhagen's Kastrup airport will soon be 45 years old and cannot be expanded any further, but despite its age Kastrup is a highly modern installation.

CHAPTER 10

THE PEOPLE OF COPENHAGEN

What in Germany is referred to as "Copenhagener" is called in Copenhagen "Vienna Bread". It is a Danish institution without which, life by the Sound and Baltic would be inconceivable. This "Vienna Bread" is a pastry which must be at hand at all times during the day and night, preferably still warm.

Apart from these "Copenhageners" there are those who were born here and finally those Copenhageners who, having lived for twenty years in the city, will say "I am a Fúnbo" (from the isle of Fúnbo), "I am a Jyde" (from Jutland) etc. Outwardly these two latter groups of Copenhageners are hardly different from one another. They have the same routine and way of life, whether on a bicycle, in a restaurant, swimming pool, office, at home, in the summer house, or even in the way they approach foreigners.

Only on rare occasions can you notice which of the Copenhageners originate from the province, for instance during a soccer match province versus capital. Then all those born in the province will of course cheer their team. Once a year both groups are in splendid harmony at "Idrätsparken" stadium, namely during the international against Sweden. When the home team beats the "arch enemy" they fly into one another's arms in jubilation, when the result is reverse they all sigh in harmony.

The Home of a true Copenhagener is furnished and equipped in a modern way which does not preclude a few bric-a-brac items from invading the cool modern atmosphere. Maybe some souvenirs brought back last year from the summer holiday abroad. A Copenhagen flat includes fitted cupboards, hot water, refrigerator, refuse disposal shaft, oil heating, balcony and fitted wardrobes.

Many flats having four or five rooms are in Copenhagen referred to as two-room units. This type of two-room flats was invented when the government after the war was not prepared to finance larger dwellings, but Jens and Jytte still wanted more space. One built two rooms, a kitchen, a bathroom, a reception room and two "bedrooms" and the whole thing was simply labelled a two-room unit.

Rent is high, but Jytte does not mind going to work as well so that they can afford the rent plus the summer holiday.

A good Copenhagener goes to Majorca for his summer holiday. Since Jytte helps so efficiently by taking a job herself, and continues to do so when money has long ceased to be the problem, Jens does his share at home. He washes up, cooks meals and pushes the pram. He has totally equal rights in his and Jytte's home.

After work many of the Jensens go home on their bikes, but many have long replaced the "Cykel" by a car, and those who have not got quite as far to go, by a moped, called "Knallert" (banger) because of its typical noise. The word has been officially absorbed in the Danish dictionary and you can read road signs "Knallertkørsel paa Cyclestien forbudt" (No bangers allowed on cycling track).

Those who pedal home during the afternoon on their

Absalon, founder of city 1167.

bicycle continue to enjoy the old Copenhagen privilege which reads: "Cyclists have the right of way whether he moves through the streets by his own or in a row of six abreast". An undisputed 'right of way' is held by the cycling messengers who are known for their speed, big mouths and sharp wit. A story about such a messenger boy is told from the last war. A German tank was in position in the Town Hall Square and a messenger boy had parked his bike against it. The soldier on guard did not like this and told the messenger to move his bike whereupon the latter replied: "If you are so afraid that your tank might tip over I shall of course park my bike elsewhere".

Once, there were 500,000 bicycles in Copenhagen and the number should still be the same today, but nobody knows exactly how many of these are still used. The number of the dusty veterans in the public bicycle stands and infront of houses is enormous. Once in a while the council has to organise a removal campaign for bicycles abandoned. Then heavy lorries with piles of rusty bicycles head for the scrap yards outside town.
The Copenhageners like to be in the country, and for this purpose invented the "Skovtur", the picnic in the woods. An essential requisite in this context is "Madame Bleue", a large coffee pot in blue enamel.

The site of the picnic is not too deep in the forest, nearer to the main road so that one can see other Copenhageners as they struggle to reach their Skovtur goal with Madame Bleue.

It may also be that Jens and Jytte have an allotment in which case another attribute to the blue coffee pot is a flagpole from which flies the "Danebrog" on Sundays or on the birthday of a family member.

The next step beyond the garden shed in the allotment is the Summer House of which Jens and Jytte dream. The most ideal notion is the Summer House by the seaside amidst fir trees. A nightmare is the possibility on the other hand that some visitors may drop on them without warning. If possible the whole family moves to the Summer House in spring and will not return to the city until late summer, in which case Jens and Jytte will have to commute a little further to and from the office.

Also in their city flat Jens and Jytte would not expect visitors without previous arrangement. The remark "Why don't you drop in" is neither a cliché nor a serious invitation, rather an expression of courtesy. A serious invitation sounds like this: "8 o'clock Tuesday for evening coffee". In that case you go to see them, take a few flowers along, not necessarily a big bouquet; you will be served coffee with pastry, cheese sandwiches, followed by a Sjus, a whisky soda or something similar, alternatively a few Bajer (bottles of beer).

Should the invitation read "Tuesday, 7p.m., for a snack" "et stykke mad", you better watch it, best not to eat anything at all earlier on, and as for the flowers for Jytte they may in this case be a bit more substantial. The "snack" may last for a few hours, after the first few rounds you are perfectly free to take off your jacket and sing a few songs.

Since it is almost impossible to enter a Copenhagen home without invitation the busy "Tursitraadet" Tourist Board operates a "Meet the Danes" scheme through which invitations are arranged to visit Danish families in their homes. The idea is to enable married couples from abroad to be invited for the traditional coffee after dinner, 8p.m. as a rule. The Tourist Board in their literature stress that. the invitation does not include accommodation overnight in the home of the Danish hosts. Also, would you please not bring your children along, and confine your stay to three hours. Such visits are not possible during Christmas, Easter and Whitsun holidays. These days belong to the family, meals as a rule they stretch out over a long period of time. It is equally difficult to meet the Danes at home during July and August. Young people have an opportunity of meeting young Danes through the "get together" activities of the Danish students' association, "Studenterforeningen" in Boulevard H.C. Andersen. This "get together" programme not only includes informal parties but also educational events, talks and, of course, discussions.

An invitation to the home invariably means additional work to the housewife. If Jens and Jytte could afford it they would rather invite their guests to join them at some restaurant; there are those who can afford it, but they are in the minority.

In the circumstances one makes discomfort a virtue and organises a "bottle party", so called "Sammenskudsgilde" with all expenses shared. At the conclusion of a true "Sammenskudsgilde" the men find themselves in the kitchen trying to put everything in the world right. This turns out sometimes to be such great fun that it becomes the starting point of another party.

The Danes have an approach to living which is extremely attractive, even in their soberest moments they are almost completely free from repression. They are equally hard-working and cheerful and extract a full measure of enjoyment from each passing day.

You can converse with the average Copenhagener in several languages, even in Danish, although it is rather difficult to persuade most of them to refrain from using their excellent English, and speak their native language. It is not all that difficult to uncover the secrets of the Danish language. If you are in doubt as to the correct ending of a word, simply swallow it. Anyhow, to start a conversation a single word works wonders, namely "Tak" which means "Thank you". You say "Tak" to fill any gap of a conversation, you say it whenever you receive something or give something, when you ask for the bill, after you have said it, when you ask a question or answer it, or even when you don't get an answer. You say "Tak" when you get-up or lie down, you say it in the lounge, the kitchen, the bedroom, by land, sea and air.

"Tak" plays an important part when you visit somebody. You use it by the front door, in the cloak room, at the table, when you leave, you say "tak" to the husband, the wife, the other guests, you say "Thank you for a nice evening", and the following day you say "thank you for yesterday". When you meet any of the "Thank you" sayers, you say "Tak for sidst", Thank you for the last time. Jytte and Jens will say "Tak" during an evening at least as many times as you and yet they would be surprised if the guest does not ring-up the following day to say "Tak for i gaar" (Thank you for yesterday), they would wonder where they went wrong and displeased their guests.

An important place within the family is occupied by the children; it is so important that the guest is not expected to show any astonishment or make any remarks about the fact that little "so and so" is still climbing over tables or chairs at a late hour. In such cases it is better to confine one's comments to "What a nice boy he is" or the like. You show consideration to children, they are smaller and therefore more in need of protection. This is why elderly ladies would sometimes get-up in the streetcar to offer their seat to Jytte's youngest.

Time for a beer in the Tivoli.

CHAPTER 11

FOOD

Eating in Copenhagen is also a vitally important fact of life, which in this case is attended to with much indulgence, time and colourful variation.

It is not true though, to say that Copenhageners spend a great deal of their time devising new recipies. It is true however, that they don't eat to live but live in order to enjoy good food and drink. To achieve this goal there are a few rules: you don't gobble your food down, but take your time, you also enjoy it visually, colour must also be on the table, flowers, figurines, candles, ribbons. The range of dishes is very wide indeed, from a slice of rye bread with a baked potato to the lengthy list of Smørrebrød, that is a piece of bread spread with butter on which the Danes pile an assortment of fish and meat together with pickles of various descriptions. Some of these smørrebrød specialities bear household names like "The Vet's Supper". There is simple "beer soup" and colossal joints of juicy roast beef and pork, crisp and mouthwatering, from which you don't cut thin slices, but virtually carve-off a handsome piece.

There are three to five meals a day, while coffee breaks are even more frequent. Also beer is not unpopular by any means, nobody minds on the other hand if in a restaurant someone orders a glass of milk to go with his meal. The day starts with the Early Morning Coffee, a cup of coffee with "Rundstykker" and "Franskbrød",

rolls and wheat bread, marmalade, cheese and some sausage. You get through the morning as a rule without further mealbreaks, but at 12 noon there is breakfast, also called "lunch" in modern Danish. You may bring along your Frokost in the sandwich box and eat it sitting on the base of a fountain, but you may also sit at an enormous table in a comfortable armchair. If you go to a restaurant, you can ask for a smørrebrød order form, alternatively order an "Anrichtung" or make use of that astonishing Danish institution known as "Cold Buffet" (Koldt Bord).

On the Smørrebrød Form you tick whatever combination you would like. There are three columns on the form for bread, rye bread, wheat bread or toast. At the left margin you find the various sandwiches listed from fresh shrimps, salmon, varied species of herring, roast beef with onions, topped by a fried egg, to cheese.

The check list varies in length from one place to another. The longest one exists at Oskar Davidsen in Gyldeløvesgade which lists almost two hundred different smørrebrød varieties. You can make your choice at leisure, nobody will rush you. Three smørrebrød per person is par, a hungry tourist will hardly be able to cope with more at a time.

With your smørrebrød you drink snaps and beer which in many cases will cost more than the food itself. If you want to drink something less expensive take "lys Pilsner" which is a "Lager" and less strong than its powerful brother, but hardly different in taste.

If you order an "Anrichtung" you are spared the trouble of marking the check list, the food is served on an enormous plate which is placed on a rack on the table. This rack is so high that a beer bottle just about fits underneath it. There are small "Anrichtungs" and large ones, the latter amount to a banquet with dozens of various dishes. Also here you start with fish, followed by cold meat and sausage, salads, hot dishes and finally cheese. With your fish and cheese you drink a snaps, that is at least one. And to finish the whole session you drink coffee and cognac. Another alternative is "Det Store Kolde Bord" (the large Cold Buffet) which holds away at lunch time and is a Danish breakfast of the third order. You are confronted with an enormous table at the centre of the room which you may approach from all sides and from which you may pick whatever and as much as you like, so long as you don't push your neighbour. The quality of the Large Cold Buffet varies, so do the prices.

A famous buffet is at Hotel Royal, on the 21st floor high above Central Railway Station, where "Denmark Luncheon" is served at noon and "Candlelight Dinner" in the evening which means you get also a demonstration of how the Danes lay the table.

Most important rule if you want to survive all these pleasures: take your time, enjoy at leisure and don't charge into the fray too recklessly. In recent years a certain type of modern "self service" restaurant has become very popular for quick lunches. They offer an international choice but include of course also Medisterpølse, Rullepølse Fläskesteg. The Danes eat their dinner around 6p.m., so they can go out on a spree, or just out, that much earlier. Danish dinner specialities are pork, "Kasseler" called Hamborgerryg by the Danes, or Filet Steak (Mørbraten) or a juicy Fransk Bøf, a beef steak.

The meat comes to the table as a joice in each case. National desserts are apple tart and a special red pudding. The late evening coffee plays an important part in daily routine, it is normally served at 9p.m. You cannot do without it.

In alphabetical order the Danish menu and list of food ranges from A to Ø, for this is the last letter in the Danish alphabet.

<u>Aalborger</u> is the citizen of Aalborg but also the name of an Aquavit which is made there, and has won for many years many golden and silver medals at international exhibitions.

<u>Bacon</u> is one of the most important export goods of

Denmark as we all know. For the sake of this bacon a special pig species was bred with a rib longer than other pigs.

Bilksemad is available in every reasonably managed Copenhagen butcher shop. It is a mixture of meat cubes, potatoes, onions of various descriptions, prepared in the frying pan makes a tasty and inexpensive meal.

Bajer is not a Bavarian but a bottle of beer.

Cheery Heering is a liqueur made from a special morello cherry variety grown in south Zealand. The liqueur takes its name after the owner of the distillery, Mr. Heering.

Dyr means deer, a Dyresteg is a venison steak.

Enebär is juniper from which Enebär rum is made.

Efterspil is the "afterplay" the cup of coffee in the house of a friend on the way home in the small hours of the morning or, alternatively, the last glass of beer, "one for the road".

Frikadeller which in English would be described as "Hamburgers" but in fact are in Denmark a matter of national pride, they must be prepared and fried as "mother used to do".

Forloren Hare would be equivalent to a "meat loaf", a solid popular dish which in Denmark is invariably eaten with a brown sauce although many foreigners will be wondering why the Copenhageners are so crazy about this brown gravy.

Forloren Skildpadde is a mockturtle which you can buy in many shops wrapped in foil so that you can cook them at home without first unwrapping them.

Grønsager stands for vegetables which is served without spices, gravy or other ingredients.

Gule Arter are yellow peas and are in high esteem, they are part of the agricultural history of the country.

Hummer is lobster, very popular and expensive.

Is is icecream which is sold everywhere in the city in all varieties and colours.

Jordbaer, the strawberry has in Copenhagen even an establishment of its own, an old coffee-house in Strøget referred to as strawberry cellar; as you enter you may have to bend down a little.

Krydder are round, tasty biscuits which, spread thick with butter are part and parcel of the early morning coffee.

Kryddersild is a specially prepared herring snack which in this quality exists only in Denmark. Here many old recipes exist to prepare it.

Laks is salmon, slightly smoked and eaten as an hors d'oeuvre with toast.

Leverpostej is liver pate, for some Danish housewives this is a sort of qualification criterium. In the butchers it is on sale in enormous quantities sufficient to satisfy a whole community. It is one of the basic food items in Denmark.

"Mälk gir Sundhed" Milk is good for you, as it reads on many houses in Denmark. With these large poster four flies were caught with one stroke: firstly it is effective publicity, secondly the orders helped Danish artists, thirdly a number of ugly end walls were beautified and fourthly the slogan is even true.

Napolens Kage Napoleon's gateaux is filled with cream, fruit, whipped cream and covered with icing sugar.

Oksebryst breast of beef with horseraddish, belongs to every genuine smørrebrød platter.

Pandekager in Copenhagen mainly denotes Town Hall Pancakes. During official functions the council serve their guests a special variety of pancakes which are made according to a secret recipe. It is believed that whisky plays a certain part in these town hall pancakes.

Rejer are crabs, the larger ones from Greenland, the smaller ones, which are the best, from Roskilde Fjord. They are eaten on white bread or toast with lemon or pepper. Rejer are in the upper price range of foodstuffs.

Sigterbrød is ordered if you don't want either white bread or rye bread, it is an in-between.

Torsk is a swear word, but also the traditional haddock on New Year's eve.

Table Manners are rather liberal as well.

Vienna Bread is a handy entremese at all times during day and night.

AE is the secondlast letter in the Danish alphabet. Able is the apple which is a most versatile ingredient on the Danish menu from apple sauce to apple strudel.

Ø concludes the alphabet and in terms of eating this can only mean oil: Beer or Øllebrod med Flødeskum is Beer soup with whipped cream.

CHAPTER 12

THE SURROUNDING COUNTRYSIDE
AND THE ØRE SOUND

Copenhagen has long burst its original seams. If you want to use a contemporary expression you would say that the surroundings have become an integral part of the city's townscape. Copenhagen is a region which embraces the whole of north Zealand and stretches about 30 miles to the west and south, and today even across the Sound. The "Øre Sound region" and the conglomeration on both sides of the Sound has also been given a new name of its own: Ørestad. More than twenty Million people cross the Sound every year and by 1980 the figure is expected to reach the forty million mark. At the moment most of the twenty million are carried by boats which operate a permanent shuttle service between Copenhagen and north Zealand on the Danish coast and Limhamn and Hälsinborg on the Swedish coast. Before the year 2000 the total figure of Sound passengers is expected to increase up to fifty million, who hopefully will no longer have to rely on a ferry service but will be able to use a bridge for their crossing. For many years study groups have carried out research work into the best possible site for the first bridge across the Sound. The most likely solution at the moment looks like a road link between Copenhagen and Malmö via the isle of Saltholm where the new big north European airport is to be built. Part of this link is planned as a tunnel whilst the remaining part is to be a bridge. An additional railway and road bridge is planned for a later stage between Helsingør and Hälsingborg in the north at the narrowest point of the Sound. The towns and villages of the Øre Sound region lead a life of their own, they levy their own local tax and each one of them would like to preserve its local character. They shall continue to do so in future according to the hopes and opinions of the planners. Køge lies to the South of Copenhagen, along national highway No.2. The route follows the coastline, but you don't see much of the Baltic because the road is lined almost continually with one summer house after another, or fir-tree nurseries planted in sandy soil. There are a few spots where also those who have no summer house will find a stretch of beach for a swim, but it is advisable to choose the officially allocated areas although the beach is open to everyone. In the Køge Bay there is no single coherent beach, anyway the water is rather shallow at some points and consequently there is not much scope for swimming here.

Køge is a small town which the hurried traveller misses easily if on the bypass. There is hardly another town in Zealand which boasts more ancient half-timbered houses, the oldest ones date back to the 16th century. They are in Kirkestraede; by the market square are the Vaevergaarden (1634) and the mayor's house. There is also a museum at Køge devoted to local history of the area. Some 19 miles from the capital you come to Roskilde, Zealand's second largest city, old, famous and regal. A thousand years ago Roskilde was both the king's and the bishop's town. Later it handed over both titles to Copenhagen. Today Roskilde is a busy industrial town with an 800 year old cathedral at the centre; the cathedral bears Romanesque and Gothic features, the spires date back to 1635. Most of Denmark's kings have found their final resting place here, together with the only queen the country ever had during the past. Significantly enough her name was also Margrete; she was the mighty ruler of Denmark, Norway and Sweden who in 1397 signed the Kalmar Union, an ill-started attempt to unite Scandinavia under one ruler.

Apart from numerous treasures of art there is one particularly interesting object within the cathedral, a 500 year old clock and a pillar on which many Danish and foreign monarchs have marked their heights, including Peter the Great and the Duke of Windsor.

The surroundings of Roskilde are also worth a visit; Ledreborg palace near Lejre is a Baroque building dating back to 1740; the palace chapel and park are open to the public. A reconstruction of the past is carried out in the Historical Archaeological Research Centre where you can even find an iron-age village on the open ground. Vigen Strandpark is a vast camping site less than 3 miles from the town centre. Another 3 miles to the east is Vidinge Natural Park, the Atomic Research Establishment is on the peninsula of Risø, not open to the public, but you can see it from Highway 6.

Very modern is the Viking Ship Museum near the harbour. The exhibits were salvaged by the National Museum from the Fjord near Roskilde.

Mediaeval finds and equipment are on show in Roskilde Museum. St. Jørgensbjerg Church dates back to approximately 1100.

North Zealand, the north of Copenhagen, is the favourite "hinterland" of the Copenhageners where they go for an outing, or even a whole season. It is also the area where Summer Houses fetch and cost maximum prices. The charm of north Zealand is manyfold: vast woods with Denmark's national tree, the beech, rolling hills and meadows, thatched houses, craggy cliffs and sandy beaches, idyllic small towns and lakes, and of course the open sea, the Kattegat.

The Coastal Road from Copenhagen to Helsingør leads through the most expensive part of North Zealand, it is lined with the villas of the most affluent Copenhageners and by the back door the most luxurious yachts are moored. The road runs immediately along the Sound and was therefore nicknamed "the Danish Riviera". There is not much open building land left on the 30 miles stretch.

As you leave Copenhagen you first reach Klampenborg with its length of man-made sandy beach which during the summer is packed out like the French Riviera. On the other side of the road is the Deer Park Dyrehave.

A very posh sanatorium is at Skodsborg whilst Nivaa houses an art gallery with paintings by German, Flemish and French masters among them Rembrandt and Rubens. (Open 1p.m. - 4p.m. - Sunday, Wednesday, Friday, from 15th May to 15th September).

Part of the Danish corniche are also the various sailing and yachting harbours, an 18-hole Golf Course exists at Rungsted.

The Louisana Museum is at Humlebäk. As you approach the modern Hotel Kystens Perle in Snekkersten the first landmark of Helsingør appears on the horizon, the silhouette of Kronborg Castle.

But Helsingør has more to offer than Kronborg; to millions it is known as the biggest entrance and exit gate of Denmark. The crossing with the ferryboat to Sweden takes only 20 minutes and runs from 6.45a.m. to midnight. You need not worry about the frequency or whether to book unless you have an appointment. There will shortly be another boat even when you can still see the stern of the previous one as it leaves through the harbour passage. You will notice a lot of heavy marine traffic going in a North-South direction through the Sound. Denmark made a lot of money from this traffic during the period 1426 to 1857 by levying Sound Dues. Helsingør in particular benefited from it, because it was here that these dues were collected. The centuries of the dues were the town's most profitable years, this is not only evident in the form of the Kronborg castle but also the many old houses within the town, particularly in Strandgade by the harbour.

The Church of St. Mary and the adjoining Carmelite Monastery date back to the late middle ages. This is the best preserved monastery in Scandinavia, and the west wing contains the Elsinor Museum.

The Marienlyst Palace in the northern outskirts of the town houses the Hamlet and Sound Dues Museum.

Modern Helsingør lives off it's trade and industry. The biggest industry is the shipbuilding yards within the harbour area. There is also a good beer brewed in Helsingør, one of its labels being of course "Hamlet". For the tourists there are big and small hotels, the biggest owned by a man who calls his chain "the festival corner of the North". In this festival corner you can rent a bridal suite with many mirrors, play Roulette, have a swim in the seawater basin of the indoor swimming pool, sweat off your excess in the sauna, go to the theatre, brood by the late-night bar, and have all sorts of other entertainment. Marienlyst has also a 12-hole golf course.

If you leave Helsingør in a north-westerly direction the road will lead to Denmark's most popular seaside places. Along this coastline a vast holiday resort has developed during the last two decades. Numerous summer-house villages have sprung up and it is regarded very "in" to spend the summer season here. A trip along this coast presents a panorama in which idyllic scenes alternate with natural grandeur. Grazing cows on the green of the rolling hills contrast with craggy cliffs on the other side. Not far from a little lake you can stand by the open sea which is virtually without a horizon; during the summer, the sunsets on the surroundings in a red which can hardly be exceeded in colour intensity.

After you have passed through Hellebäk you reach Aalsgaarde, a small idyllic place. A few miles further, where the coast opens up and you can see the Swedish peninsula of Kullen on the other side, lies one of Denmark's best reputed seaside resorts: Hornbäk. It has had this reputation for quite some time. The place is a mixture of a fishermen's village and a fashion show. The yachting harbour, or rather its contents, represents an astounding concentration of capital. The beaches and dunes here are first-class. The vast "plantation" by the coast was laid-out as early as 150 years ago. From the viewing points "Ørnereden" (eagle's nest) and "Kaptajnens Bänk" (Captain's bench) you enjoy a magnificent view far out over the Kattegat. In Kildekrog, near Hornbäk, there is a museum containing sculptures and paintings by the Danish artist Rudolph Tegner.

The next place of any consequence is Gilleleje, at the northern tip of the coast, this is also a fishermen's village and seaside resort.

Then the coast turns to the south-west. Before you reach Hundested (from where you can cross to west Zealand and Jutland) there are many more miles of sandy beaches and rocky cliffs at Raageleje, Vejby, Tisvildeleje, Liseleje, all with innumerable summer houses and flag-poles. At Tisvilde Hegn and Asserbo Plantage, the latter with the ruins of a very old castle, you can enjoy extensive walks through woods full of variation as far as the growth is concerned.

In the north-west corner of Zealand there is a small but equally important industrial town: Frederiksvärk, where you have the only steel mill in Denmark. Almost one third of all the steel consumed in the country is made here with the use of scrap. In 1756 Major General J.F. Classen started a gunpowder factory and a foundry at Frederiksvärk. The walls of the present foundry still date back to these days, and are more than 3ft. thick.

The route from Frederiksvärk to Copenhagen leads via Hillerød, the heart of North Zealand. Not only is the big Frederiksborg castle a landmark of the town but so are its' small houses lining the gently curved streets, the lake and it's wooded surroundings. The palace park is laid out in the French style, with broad straight avenues and accurately lopped box-trees. To the west of the Palace is a small country-seat which Frederik II had built for himself.

Travelling from Hillerød in a northern direction you reach the Gribskov Woods, Denmark's second largest forest. When the beeches break into leaf and the first green of spring appears, thousands of Copenhageners head for the Gribskov area. Incidentally the mushrooms you get here in the autumn have the same effect. If there is a lasting snowfall during the winter the Copen-hageners even come ski-ing here because of the hills and slopes. On the eastern outskirts of the forest lies Lake Esrom with the Fredensborg Palace on the other bank. This is still used as a royal residence during the spring and autumn seasons. The road from Hillerød to Copen-hagen is one of the fastest in the country, and one of the prettiest as well. Forest alternates with modern residential areas. People like to live here in the north-west of the big city and you can almost define Hillerød as a suburb of Copenhagen. You get an idea as to how many Copenhageners live here when you travel on this road during the rush hour.

Near Holte, halfway between Hillerød and Copenhagen, is Rude Skov, one of the most beautiful forests in Zealand, with Lake Løgsø and Lake Agersø and the commanding viewing point of Høje Sandbjerg. The heights of Holte are also famous for another reason, at least within Denmark. Here the Danish ski-jumping championships are held every winter. With modest reference to the Norwegian Holmenkollen ski-jumping event high above Oslo, the Copenhageners call their slope "Holtekollen". If there is not sufficient snow they simply have it transported from Norway by freight-train.

Between Holte and Lyngby is the Sorgenfri palace with the open air museum.

The Sorgenfri Palace which was built in 1705, is the residence of the late king's brother, Prince Knud, who was born in 1900.

Here to the north of the city is also Denmark's most popular regatta course: Bagsvärd Sø.

CHAPTER 13

IN SCANIA

During the German occupation traffic from Copenhagen across the Sound assumed a quite particular significance. The Danes used this route to smuggle fellow countrymen whose lives were at risk of the Nazis, out of the country to neutral Sweden. After the war the Swedish cinemas had a great part in the further development of the cross Sound service. Due to a quarrel between American distributors and Danish cinemas over the percentage to be paid, the American superfilms did not reach Denmark, but they were on show on the other side of the Sound. At that time a young Copenhagener who is said to have had little more than 50 Øre in his pocket, had the idea to organise special cinema trips between Tuborg Harbour and Landkrona, using chartered boats. For 15 Kroner you could cross, enjoy Scarlett in "Gone with the Wind" and drink duty-free snaps on the boat, the latter of course was not included in the 15 Kroner. The success of these cinema trips was so great that soon two boats were in service, modified ex-German mine-layers, which were eventually bought by the operators and in a sense of gratitude named Scarlett. One day the quarrel of the film people had come to an end and, with it, the cinema excursions.

But there have always been and still are other attractions on either side of the Sound. The Swedes like to enjoy themselves in Copenhagen and buy foodstuffs, the Danes buy goods on the other side such as textiles; those who know their way around, make sufficient bargains that they virtually cover the expenses of their passage, and that does include duty-free pleasures of various kinds. The finance ministers of both countries agreed a few years ago that spirits bought on the boat are not permitted to be taken ashore. You have to consume them aboard ship. The results of this regulation are clearly visible and audible in Havnegade where most Sound ferries moor. It has also been alleged that some passengers don't even bother to leave the boat but stay aboard and go straight back. There is also good food on the boat.

You could of course also make the crossing in order to go sightseeing, and enjoy the country of Scania. It has been said that, once you know this Swedish province, you know the whole of Sweden. Here you find the most fertile farmland, deep woods, sandy beaches, cliffs and rocks, in other words the full range of Swedish scenery.

Originally Scania was not Swedish at all; together with the provinces of Blekinge and Halland it belonged to Denmark until 1658, when by the Peace Treaty of Roskilde they were separated from Denmark and incorporated into Sweden. The People of Scania are looked upon in Sweden as a quite particular group, a sort of minority. There is the saying: I am not Swedish, I am Scanian. Equally peculiar is the dialect spoken in Scania which reflects clearly Danish linguistic elements, it is the most difficult-to-understand Swedish that ever existed.

The crossing from Helsingør to Hälsingborg takes twenty minutes, from Copenhagen to Malmö just under 100 minutes, but the hydrofoils make it in 35 minutes. You can combine conventional and modern way of travelling, that is go by hydrofoil and come back on a larger boat. An evening programme of this type covers three and half hours. But you can of course stay longer in Scania, there is lots to see.

The famous Round Tower built by Christian IV in the 17th century.

Malmö is the third largest city in Sweden, it grows and expands constantly with a population at present of 250,000; if you include the increasingly "urbanised" environs you arrive at 350,000. There is a pronounced self-confidence in the Malmö region beside the two big brothers Stockholm and Göteborg. There are people at Malmö who in all modesty predict that in a few years time Malmö will be the capital of Scandinavia, a central meeting point. This self-confidence may be rooted in history because during the 16th century Malmö was as big as Copenhagen and much bigger than Stockholm "up there at the end of the world".

The people of Scania are not only proud but also very efficient. A sense of well-being strikes you as soon as you set foot in this city of industry, commerce and seafare.

As you approach the coast from the Sound the first part of Malmö you notice, are three towering chimneys. They belong to Scandinavia's biggest steam-operated power plant and stand 280 ft. high. You can also see the installation of Kockums shipbuilding yards where ships up to 300,000 tons can be built, the latest dock is 1300 ft. long. Malmö has well managed hotels, a 4½ mile long sandy beach, vast parks, modern building blocks, old half-timbered houses, a Trade Fair and sports grounds which are well known, throughout Europe. If you want to enjoy a panoramic view of the city in comfort go to the "Oversten" (the Colonel) which is a restaurant on the 26th floor of the "Kron-prinsen" (crown prince) centre. You are on a site where once a colonel was in charge, that was in the barracks of the Swedish Crown Prince's regiment, which after the war gave way to a totally non-military residential and shopping centre, still referred to as the "Kronprinsen".

Kronprinsen is a vertical city of its won in which you can live from birth to death without ever having to leave it. Everything you need for living is available within the Kronprinsen. Doctors, national insurance offices, amenities for amusement, entertainment and sport, even a TV station of their own. The only thing you cannot have in Kronprinsen is your funeral. 3000 people live at Kronprinsen in 770 dwellings added to which there are another 2000 who come everyday to work. The underground car park can accommodate 1200 cars.

Kronprinsen is quite a sight from the architectural point of view. The high building appears elegant, maybe because its facade starts off in a dark blue at the bottom and gradually blends into an increasingly lighter blue, it grows into the sky and has not simply been forced into it.

Malmö has a first-class gastronomic reputation. There is hardly another Swedish city where you could find more and better eating places. They include quaint establishments with equally idyllic names such as the "Witch Chamber" in the old town hall, restaurant "Hyllie 19" which is tucked away in an old 1809 farmhouse in the Hyllie district out of town (streetcar No.4), or restaurants "Tunneln" and "Kockska Krogen" in mediaeval houses where the ceiling is so low at places that you have to bend down as you walk by. The biggest top-level restaurants are the "Savoy" and the "Kramer".

There are also various interesting historic sights in Mälmo. St. Peter's church and the Mälmohus castle date back to the 14th century. "Flensburg House" at No.9, Södergatan is 16th century, a charming building in late Renaissance style. Jörgen Kocks House at No.2 Västergatan, was built in 1525. Its first occupant, Jörgen Kock, was burgermaster, banker and a very rich man. He governed the city singularly for three decades. He was a sly fox, so they say, but he must have been a philantropic fox. He left a substantial trust for the poor, those in need and schoolchildren.

In Kompanigatan which branches off the market square, is the 16th century Kompaniehuset. At No. 24, Baltzarsgatan we find Claus Mortensens Hus. Mortensen was the leader of the reformation movement in Malmö. Further old houses are Rosenvingska Huset at No.5, Västergatan and "Apoteket Lejonet" (an old Apotheker's house) in the big market square, the latter in Dutch Renaissance style.

Only 6 miles from Malmö lies Lund, almost 1000 years old, the famous university town and old religious capital. The city was founded in 1020 by King Canute the Great, but even before that time there was a market here.

The cathedral of Lund is Scandinavia's biggest building in

Romanesque style, it was consecrated in 1145. The crypt is even of an earlier date, namely 1123. The astronomical clock which still plays daily at noon, is six hundred years old, also there is an altar shrine which originates from around 1400.

Adjoining the cathedral is Lundagaard Park in which you find Kungshuset or Lundagaardshuset. The 16th century red-brick building was erected as a residence for King Frederik II of Denmark. Later on it became a university until in 1882 the new main university building nearby was completed. The Lund university was founded in 1662, today it enrols 15,000 students the city's population is 50,000. Widely known are also Lund's Botanical Gardens with more than 7000 plant species and cultivations.

Further to the north by the Sound lies Landskrona another "oppsoite number" of Copenhagen. The boats to Landskrona sail from Tuborg Havn. Landskrona has been a city in its own right since 1413. The 16th century fortifications surrounding the castle are rated as the best preserved relics of their kind in Europe and give us some idea as to what was going on in those days around the Sound. At one time the mediaeval town was gutted by fire and a new town was built on land reclaimed from the sea. Buildings in the Classic style of this period have been preserved: Sofia Albertina church, Fortifikationshuset at No. 4, Parkgatan, Haijska Huset at No. 13, Kungsgatan where Selma Lagerlöf wrote her Gösta Berling. Selma Lagerlöf was a teacher in Landkrona from 1885 to 1895.

From Landskrona you can cross to the isle of Hven in the middle of the Sound; Hven became famous with the Danish astronomist Tycho Brahe who worked here during the 16th century in a sort of exile. From this period Uraniborg Renaissance palace and Stjärneborg Observatory have been preserved. Nearby is the Tycho Brahe Museum. St. Ibb church on the hillside of Backafallen in the west of the island dates back to the 13th century.

The Swedish town nearest to Denmark is Hälsinborg, less than 3 miles from Helsongør at the narrowest point of the Sound. Here you find the traffic on the Sound at its busiest. If you climb a few hundred yards from the harbour you reach a mediaeval tower stronghold known as Kärnan (the Keep) which together with the castle, was once used to guard the passage to, and from the Sound. This was a Danish castle and you are reminded here, that this was precisely what caused the anger of other European rulers. Namely that the Danes had dug their heels in deeply on both sides of the Sound. This enabled them to fill the coffers so successfully with the Sound Dues. Utimately this was the reason why nobody came to their rescue when the Swedes took from them Blekinge, Halland, Scania, and even Bornholm; the latter was liberated however a few years later and "placed back into the hands of the Danish King". Not far from the harbour is St. Mary's church, built in the 13th century and rebuilt during the 15th century; it has an interesting triptych and a magnificent late Renaissance pulpit.

The shopping streets of Halsinborg are an ideal combination of modern efficiency and leisurely restfulness. Many pedestrians and no cars, but benches and flowers in front of modern shops.

If you have a little more time to spare on your excursion from Copenhagen across the Sound, take a closer look at Scania inland. You will soon realise how logical the project-planners are in their conception to turn this area into a vast holiday resort for the tormented people of Ørestad.

North of Hälsinborg is the peninsula of Kullen with it's various summer resorts. The Swedish king has a summer palace near Hälsinborg.

In the south of Scania two towns are in rivalry as to which one is the Southernmost in Sweden: Trelleborg and Ystad. It is wise not to mention the name of the other town when you visit either of them. Trelleborg is an important Baltic seaport whilst Ystad is a mediaeval city which believes in a great future as a tourist centre. One of the most remarkable ancient buildings is St. Maria Church, begun in the early 13th century as a basilica in Romanesque style, but incorporating many additions of a later date. There is a ferry service to Bornholm, and more recently also to Swinemunde and Kolberg. Not far from Ystad is Backaakra, an old farm which Dag Hammarskjöld bought in 1957. He arranged for it to be restored according to his own design and had planned to live here in retirement every year from spring to September. He did not live to see his plans come true.

But Dag Hammerskjöld's project has been carried out. Today the estate is a memorial place in honour of the great Swede and cosmopolite. Many personal belongings of the former UN Secretary General are displayed at Backaarka. According to his will the estate is used for two months every year by the Swedish Academy for holiday purposes.

In the north and north-east of Scania you soon enter a very idyllic forest and lake district where once upon a time robbers and thieves used to ambush travellers. Today this no longer happens, much to the relief of the tour operators.

There are quite a few castles and convents worth a visit: Bosjökloster a former Benedictine convent dating back to 1080, used now for exhibitions of modern art. Svaneholm 18 miles east of Malmö, is one of the most peculiar castles of the early 15th century. Then there is the Christinehof Palace north-west of Eljaröd, which during the two hundred years since it was built, has never been altered or modernised.

There are also thriving towns inland which welcome visitors: Hässelholm and the charming Kristianstad which still carries the initials of its founder in its coat of arms, namely Christian IV. Kristianstad has on its' east side a quaint, hidden harbour and seaside resort: Aahus.

Hässelholm lies in the Göinge district where the "robbers" lived. There are also many relics of earlier times in this area.

CHAPTER 14

HINTS FOR TOURISTS

Arrival, Information, Formalities.

Information on arrival is readily and reliably available from the friendly ladies of the Tourist Board, first corner on your right as you leave the Central Railway Station; address: No.7, Banegaardspladsen.

As a citizen of non-EEC countries you may stay in Denmark up to three months without a visa or permit. To enter the country all you need is a valid passport. Visitors from other Scandinavian countries do not need

Visitors from other Scandinavian countries do not need any documents at all. Since Denmark joined the EEC together with the U.K. and others, British citizens can now also take up employment without a special permit. The arrival of a foreigner must be reported to the local police within 24 hours, the same applies for any change of address. In hotels this formality is taken care of by the management, if you live on your own or in private accommodation you have to do this yourself. The relevant forms are available from post offices and police stations. Babysitters are available through the Women

Students' Organisation; 4A, Martensen Allee, Telephone VESTER 30 38. Banks are open from 9.30a.m. - 3 p.m., Tuesday and Friday also from 4.30p.m. - 6p.m. They are closed on Saturday. There is a bank at Central Railway Station which is open every day.

Brochures of all descriptions are available from the Information Centre at Central Railway Station. You can even obtain instruction sheets on how to prepare smørrebrød and how to use a telephone in Copenhagen.

Bicycles continue to be a very popular means of transport in Copenhagen. If you don't bring your own bicycle you can hire one at No.157, Gothersgade or at No.8, Rungsgade. If you want to ride a moped (or "Kanllert" - banger) you have to be at least 21. The bicycle must be locked whenever it is left unattended. Half an hour after sunset you have to switch the lights on. Camping, there are almost 500 camping sites in Denmark which are supervised. They are listed in an official index which you can buy for 5 Kroner from the Tourist Board offices, in bookshops or at the border. Various categories are marked in the index by asterisks. One asterisk means: basic requirements in terms of drinking water supply, terrain and sanitary installations are met. Two asterisks indicate that the site is sheltered against wind and that shopping facilities exist within a 2 kilometre radius. Three asterisks denote top quality: sanitary installations must be "A1", you can buy food supplies on the site, the site is fenced-in and there is an attendant. A total of 15 camping sites exist in and around Copenhagen.

Car Hire: to hire a car you must be at least 21. A wide range from VW to Mercedes is available. Charge per hour (minimum three hours) 7 to 22 Kroner, per day - 34-110 Kroner, per week - 205-660 Kroner. Added to this sum is 40 to 110 Øre per kilometre plus VAT. You can also hire a chauffeur-driven car.

Exhibitions, the main exhibition centres are Bella Centrat on Bellahöj and the Forum at Julius Thomsens Plads where during the winter the "Six Days" are held, a crude entertainment during which beer plays an important part to the spectators.

Guided Tours — Breweries. Breweries play an important

"Stroeget" Copenhagen's pedestrians only street.

part for the visitor to Copenhagen. The two big ones, Carlsberg and Tuborg, don't mind at all when you peep into their vats and bottling plants. They even give free beer to the visitors.

Carlsberg Brewery, at No. 100, Vester Faelledej, organise guided tours for tourists at 9a.m., 11a.m. and 2.30p.m., Monday to Friday.

Tuborg at No. 54, Strandvej, can be visited any time between 8.30a.m. and 2.30p.m. on Weekdays, and between 8.30a.m. and 10.30a.m. on Saturday. To visit other specific installations tours are organised under a respective motto; there is "Social Tour" or "Tomorrow's World". On these you visit nursery schools, schools, allotments etc. The tour starts daily, except Saturday and Sunday, at 9.15a.m. at the Town Hall Square and lasts 2" hours. Price: 23 Kroner. During the "Art and Artisan" Tour you visit silversmiths' workshops, the Royal Porcelain Manufacture, a furniture exhibition and the "Permanent Sales Exhibition". The tour takes place everyday from 1p.m. to 3.45p.m., except Saturday and Sunday. Price: 25 Kroner. Departure as above.

Hotels, the hotels in Denmark's capital are numerous and range from the most luxurious down to the very plain and modest side-street hotel. The expensive hotels are in the foreground in Copenhagen, but there are also first-class, reasonably priced hotels, only you have to book well in advance. During the off-season many hotels, especially the new ones, lower their rates to almost half the normal charge. When making a reservation it is advisable to have the prices confirmed.

Copenhagen's hotels match any international standard which is evident by the wide range of their prices. You can have a single-bedroom in a private hotel for 30 Kr. if it has not already been taken, and you can have a suite for 500 Kr. in d'Angleterre at Kongens Nytorv, provided this, too, has not already been booked. Such super-suites are as a rule on business and government expenses and there are plenty of visitors to Copenhagen who in this respect are extremely resourceful. The Mission Hotels enjoy a very good reputation for quality and reasonable prices but differ from the others mainly in that they do not serve liquor whilst you can obtain beer and wine. These hotels are often fully booked particularly when the parliament, the Folketing, is in session because the MPs like to live in the mission hotels.

The so called Students' Hotels can also be recommended, they are available to the tourists during the summer, and the students during the winter. Among them is Copenhagen's second largest hotel, Egmont, with 688 beds. The Otto Mønsted Hotel Minerva has 350 beds, all single-bedrooms; from the windows you have a view of the country as well as the city. In these hotels students work as porters, receptionists, waiters and cashiers, which, together with their linguistic versatility, produces a very attractive atmosphere of its own.

Copenhagen's highest hotel buildings are the Tre Falke, which also includes a congress and culture centre; the Royal in the SAS air terminal where Mr. Khrushchev once stayed, the Hotel Europa with a view over harbour and city, and then the very latest: the Copenhagen with 900 beds. If you don't find hotel accommodation in Copenhagen during the summer season do not hesitate to look around in the countryside; there are many good hotels in the surroundings of Copenhagen.

An Official Accommodation Service exists within Central Railway Station; open 1 May to 15 September: 9a.m. - midnight everyday, 16 September to 30 September: 9a.m. - 10p.m. everyday, 1 October to 31 October: 9a.m. - 5p.m. on Weekdays, 1 November - 31 March: 9a.m. - 5p.m. Monday to Friday, 9a.m. - 12 noon on Saturday, closed on Sunday, 1 April to 30 April 9a.m. - 5p.m. on Weekdays.

Language, a true Copenhagener, when he encounters a foreigner, will speak fluent English, which he is constantly encouraged to use by the numerous American films shown in the cinemas in their original, undubbed, version. You can of course attend a language course in Danish for foreigners for which a number of facilities exist.

Museums, most museums are open from 10a.m. till 4p.m. Admission to many museums is free, in the case of the Glyptotek on Wednesday and Sunday.

Nightlife, there are no doubt noisier cities than Copenhagen by night; Tivoli closes at the stroke of midnight, also most restaurants, some of which stay open however until 2a.m. There are some 50 bars and nightclubs which close at 5a.m.

Nyhavn is the street where most of the sailors' dives are and where incidentally policemen patrol in twos. In the area behind the Nikolaj church there are small bars and dance spots where mainly young people, individualists, artists and would-be artists meet. The locals refer to this district as the "Mine Field".

You can visit the bars and nightclubs as a couple, some you can also enter singly and leave as a couple.

'Copenhagen by night' also means to admire the illuminated publicity signs at town hall square, or to stand on the Langelinie and gaze across the harbour. One of the nicest nights in Copenhagen is Midsummer Night when people dance in the town hall square. Big fires are lit in the gardens on the outskirts and along the coast. Revellers celebrate through the whole bright night, and are particularly nice to each other and sing the midsummer tune "Vi elsker vort land" (we love our country). Restaurants, there are all sorts of restaurants in Copenhagen, from the functional quick lunch, the room with velvet and bric-a-brac, the tap room, the more exquisite with silky wallpaper, the international hotel restaurant at ground level or on the 21st floor, the quaint farmhouse or forest restaurant, the café on the terrace with a view across a lake or park, also the garden restaurant with a notice by the door telling you that you may bring your own food basket.

When estimating the cost of a meal you should be aware of the fact that the price of drinks and beer may well exceed the charges for food. Beer, snaps and wine are expensive. In this respect the KAR chain of restaurants (Kvindernes alkolfrie restauranter = restaurants of the non-alcoholic women) is an interesting proposition to the tourist. They serve good food, but you can only drink a shandy or light beer, this spares the budget considerably.

There are many famous and popular names among Copenhagen's restaurants, the list of preferences will obviously vary from one patron to another; after all the selection of a restaurant where you feel comfortable and like the atmosphere is a highly personal matter. And with this reservation we present the following list:

Royal, Europa and Codan are modern restaurants with one speciality in common: a magnificent view. They are on the upper floor of their respective hotel. On the groundfloor of Hotel "Royal" is a quick-service restaurant with reasonable prices. Opposite is "Ekko Danmark" with a large grill which you can see but not smell; if you are in a greaty hurry you can sit on a stool by the bar and eat your lunch.

Oskar Davidsen is famous for its 4ft. long smørrebrød list and the Cold Buffet. Although Oskar Davidsen moved a few years ago from a quaint, old-time environment to the larger present premises at No.24, Gyldenlövesgade, the typical Danish atmosphere has been maintained. Coq d'Or in H.C. Andersen Boulevard, despite its French name, offers totally Danish gastronomy both in terms of cuisine and service.

Sea food specialities are available at Fiskehusets and Korg's Restaurants in Gammel Strand (closed Sunday).

A few yards from here is "Den Gyldne Fortun" at No.18, Ved Stranden, opposite Christiansborg. Good food, rusticated modern interior design. The former "Nationaltidende" newspaper used to be printed in this building it ceased publication in 1961 after almost 100 years. Today businessmen and politicians from the nearby parliament have their breakfast here.

The "Glyptoteket" is a very Danish restaurant opposite the museum where you can watch all-male or all-female parties indulge in gastronomic feasts behind enormous "Anrichtung" plates.

Also the restaurant within the Central Railway Station has a reputation of good food at reasonable prices; service is multilingual and friendly and you sit in comfort.

A typical Copenhagen institution is "Latiner-Kafeen". Here you meet the Copenhageners, exhausted from their shopping tour, having a snack and a glass of sherry or beer before they plunge in the busy streets again. Many of those who sit in Latiner-Kafeen have heard it's name mentioned by their grandmothers. It is in Købmagergade, which means half-way between the university and the shopping districts.

"Nimb" at No.5 Bernstorffsgade, near the Central Railway Station, has a terrace into Tivoli gardens and is most elegant, it looks like a pagoda and has dancing. You can also enjoy dancing and music along with your meal at the very elegant "Ambassadeur" at town hall square, at "Ny Rosenborg" in H.C. Andersen Boulevard and at "Bellevue" in Klampenborg. "Lorry Landsbyen" at No.7, Allégade, offers family cabaret, a roofed beer garden restaurant where a non-stop show rolls on with music, singers and variety artists.

"Syv Smä Hjem" (seven small homes) at No.4, Jernbanegade, is a delightful intimate restaurant with a first-rate wine cellar.

An altogether different atmosphere exists at "Tokanten", the Bohemians' and students' pub, on the corner of Vandkunsten square and Raadhussträde. Here you see colossal bowls of soup, reasonably priced smørrebrød, colourful wall posters and other eccentric trappings, lots of young people.

Also the "Hiviids Vinstue" at Kongens Nytorv has had its very own character for many years, mainly frequented by actors from the "Royal" across the street. Next door to the theatre at the corner Tordenskjoldsgade is "Brønnum", a hangout of actresses and balleuses from the "Royal". Very popular are the "Fortovskafe", the side-walk cafés, like "Stephan à Porta" at Kongens Nytorv or "Frascati" in the town hall square. They are amusing places for morning coffee or afternoon snack while you survey the passing stream of bikes, trams, vendors and so on.

The "Langelinie Pavillonen", which housing the Royal Yacht Club, is an excellent place for lunches, teas, dinners, and offers the most magnificent view of the harbour.

The Copenhageners also feel very much at home where they try to put on a typically British appearance. In the case of some restaurants this attempt was quite successful. There may even be some Englishmen who think the

The town hall square at night.

pub next door to Frascati or "Queen's Pub" at Hotel King Frederik in Vester Voldgade, are the nicest English-style restaurants they have seen; there is also "John Bull Pub" adjacent to Ny Teater.

Service at all these places is quick and friendly. One endeavours not to show much excitement at the fact that so many foreigners prefer Copenhagen to Majorca. There may be misunderstandings but the Copenhageners are always eager to have a go in foreign languages, if need be he may even be prepared to speak Danish to a foreigner. In the meantime one has also become more and more adjusted to the continental habit of including 15 per cent service charges with the sum of the bill. But this is by no means typically Danish because a Dane either calculates the service charge himself or he says to the waiter: "Add 15 per cent" or "The lot, please" (det hele).

Religious Services Anglican, St. Alban's English Church, Langelinie; Roman Catholic, St. Ansgar (cathedral) No. 64, Bredgade; Jewish Synagogue, No. 12, Krystalgade.

Shopping The most enjoyable shopping tour leads from Central Railway Station via Town Hall Square criss-cross through the city centre as far as Kongens Nytorv.

Opposite the Central Railway Station, in Vesterport, is "The Permanent Exhibition of Danish Handicraft and Danish Artisans", briefly referred to as the "Permanent". Here you get a fascinating overall view of Danish decorative art, you are not compelled to buy anything although there is hardly a visitor who leaves without a small parcel or without at least having placed an order. The Queen Mother and Queen are also customers of the "Permanent". On the three floors the major categroies are: furniture, gold and silverware, pottery, wood and glassware, textiles, lamps, formative art, souvenirs; there is also a special export department which arranges for the despatch of goods abroad. The "Permanent" was formed in 1931 as an association of Craftsmen and Industrial Artisans. Any Danish manufactuer, small or important, can become a member if his products have been approved by a committee whose members are elected every year by the General Assembly. The size of the company does not matter, only the quality of the products, thus the craftsman from a remote provincial town displays his works beside the products of the well-known big companies and architects. From the Permanent our route passes by "Buen" the department store and the smørrebrød shops which are open day and night, along the broad Vesterbrogade to the Town Hall Square. On the other side Europe's longest pedestrian zone begins, more than a mile long; actually it is a series of streets running eastwards from the square and collectively known as "Strøget".

This is Copenhagen's Bond Street of Fifth Avenue. Not far along Frederiksbergade, we come to the first of the five double squares the northern half of which is called Gammeltorv, and the southern Nytorv. The most interesting thing about these twin squares is the splendid fountain. Here on April 16, the Queen's birthday, children watch "the golden apples" dance on the water jets, gilded metal balls hopping up and down like a ball in a shooting gallery. You cannot explore the Strøget in a single stroll. Cheap shops alternate with the most luxurious ones, famous and unknown shops one beside another, diamonds next to glass beads, scientific works next to frivolous books, lollipops next to caviar, artificial flowers and expensive china.

In the Strøget area there are several famous and big establishments, each of them worth a separate visit: Illum, Bing & Gröndahl, the exhibition of the Royal Porcelain Manufacture, and the Magasin du Nord.

Strøget has its attractions at all seasons, during the summer you see lots of attractive Copenhagen girls walking along in fashionable dress, in December the Christmas illuminations swing across the street.

There are of course other shopping areas in Copenhagen. Many of the specialist shops are in the little lanes on the left and right of Strøget, some of them in the basement; the latter display their goods in the street or hang them above the entrance door.

Elegant shops exist also in Bredgade and St. Kongensgade on the other side of Kongens Nytorv.

In the outskirts there are modern shopping centres, the most popular is Rødovre Center near the main road to Roskilde; shops of all kinds, restaurants, bowling alleys and car parks.

In the department stores and big shops you will have no linguistic problems, everybody speaks English. The leading houses accept even foreign currency and arrange for your goods to be despatched.

If you want to please your rich aunt back home even before your return from the holidays go to Ekko Danmark and select a food gift package of Danish specialities which they then send anywhere in the world. For a price between 25 and 100 Kr. you have a choice of eight different parcels, containing liver paté, ham, oysters, crabs, caviar, sausages, bacon, cheese, sardines and the like.

Ekko Danmark also promotes Danish produce by demonstrations, films etc. Shop Opening Hours: 9 a.m. - 5.30p.m. Monday to Thursday, on Fridays most shops stay open until 7p.m. and on Saturdays until 1p.m. or 2p.m. Patisseries and smørrebrød shops also stay open in the evening and on Sundays. The shops within the Central Railway Station close at midnight.

Transportation, the quickest way to get from A to B in Copenhagen is by the S-trains, the respective stations show a capital S in their sign. The trains operate from 5a.m. until shortly before 1a.m. Tickets are sold for a single or return journey.

There are 40 bus lines and five night lines in Copenhagen. The suburbs are served on additional lines by other companies. The buses operate from 5a.m. The last buses leave the town hall square in all directions at 30 minutes past midnight precisely. The tramways have just about disappeared from the streets of Copenhagen, except for a few veterans and the No.8 line which operates in Tivoli Gardens.

A night bus service is available between 1a.m. and 2.40a.m.

Telephones, if you want to look up a name in a Copenhagen Telephone Directory you have to bear in mind that the names are arranged in a strange way. Since there are so many Jensens and Nielsens a method had to be devised to arrange them in such a manner that you can find the right one. The names are first in alphabetical order of their occupation or profession. Should you not know the occupation of the nice Copenhagener whom you met last summer in London the matter becomes a little complicated, unless you check under the category "director". Within an occupational category the Jensens are then listed in the order of their first names. Those who have no occupation at all are at the top which is interesting from the psychological point of view.

The telephone dial has numbers and letters as we used to have in England. If you want to dial a number with a prefix such as Triangle, Byen, Palais etc., dial the first two letters whereupon the operator will answer and you ask for the number. As there are few Danes who cannot count up to ten in English you will hardly have any problems, especially if you break the number down and give it as "one, two, three, four" instead of "twelve, thirty-four". The modern times have also reached Copenhagen's telephone system, already there are some six-digit telephone numbers which you can dial directly.

Young People are welcome in Copenhagen. You can see it from the numerous facilities and amenities including those for the very young; there are playgrounds with a sign "Adults admitted only when accompanied by a child". On other sites children are not compelled to play but are allowed to build whole houses, using scrap, waste timber, bricks and old nails. Such grounds are called "Skrammellegeplads" — Junk Playground. The first of these playgrounds has become famous with educationalists all over the world. Young people have become a very important factor in tourism, whether they arrive in their own car or hitch-hike, whether they have a beard or no beard. Denmark's International Student Club (DIS) have their own hostel at No.26, Skt. Hans Torv.

Studentenforeningen is a famous forum. Every year 250 different functions are held here. During the summer there are talks, discussions, films, dancing, ballet, discotheques — open until 5a.m. for students from all over the world. The motto is "International get-together". The individual events have quite revealing names such as "Flower-pot Party", "Super Mini Move-in Movie" DIS also organises courses and journeys for students. Foreign students can take part in travelling parties organised by DIS, their offices are at No.36, Skindergade.

Ungdommens Rejseburo organises tours all over Scandinavia for groups of young people and students.

Youth Hostels "Dansk Ungdoms Herberger — also admit adults; you have to produce the membership card of a Youth Hostel Organisation in your own country. Many hostels have rooms for families, you can also arrive by car. The YMCA have a hostel for soldiers and the YWCA run a hostel for women which is open from 1 May to 1 October.